BIRDIE

By

Birdie Bomar
&
Kathryn Bankston

ISBN: 0-7596-5752-1 (E-book)
ISBN: 0-7596-5753-X (Paperback)

This book is printed on acid free paper.

1stBooks - rev. 08/07/02

"Birdie Bomar" is a poignant history in its portrayal of the challenges professional women faced during the years of World War II"

-Jenny Poole
Vice President-In-Flight Service
Delta Air Lines

AUTHOR'S NOTE

Over ten years ago on a quiet Saturday afternoon in an Atlanta real estate office, Birdie Bomar and I were assigned to assist anyone who might call or come by for information to buy, sell or rent property. I knew that Birdie was a talker, but had never had first-hand experience until she opened up and started telling one funny story after another about her career as an airline stewardess. I told Birdie she ought to share her life in a book and offered my assistance. This book is the result of that innocent beginning.

Neither Birdie nor I are talented or knowledgeable about technology and those more learned may find flaws, but we would like to express our appreciation to Chuck Larson, retired Eastern Airlines captain, who patiently served as a technical advisor. In many cases names have been changed to "protect the innocent" and sometimes names could simply not be recalled. In working with Birdie many years to accumulate her experiences of long ago, I have been impressed with her ability to recall. Should any inaccuracies be noted, please know they are unintentional and we hope they will not mar your reading pleasure.

There are many kind souls, we would like to recognize for their help in the development of this book and ask the indulgence of any who have been inadvertently overlooked. First, we would like to thank the fine people at Delta who provided encouragement when the book was still in its embryonic stage: Harriet Parker, Paulette O'Donald, Susan Harrington, along with Jenny Poole, who kindly endorsed it.

Birdie wishes to thank her cousin, Bob Sanders, Alabama writer and radio personality, who provided valuable information about Birdie's home town, and particular thanks to her nephew and author of adventure novels, Scott Jones, and his wife, Vicki, who is an American Airlines stewardess. For many years, Scott has shown his loyalty to Birdie with constant care, daily filling the role of a devoted son. Special thanks go to Vicki for her help in assembling the pictures used in this book.

Those who have assisted me in this effort include The Rev. Thomas H. Conley, who recommended I contact Mary Miller, an Atlanta author who recommended 1st Books Library. Sincere thanks go to Josh Herbert, for his help in the beginning stage; thanks also to Chip and Jennifer Shelton who continued the guidance from lst Books Library. For her patient help in copying pictures, a warm thank you to Shirley Campos, at Kinko's.

Thanks to Shelly Martin, all-around technical expert for her sage advice when my computer was beyond my control, and to Suzanne Long, for providing the silhouettes of the nurse and the plane, which are used throughout the book.

Lastly, appreciation to my son, Bob, and his wife, Lea, for their encouragement through the years, and heartfelt thanks to my sister, Mary Pallotta, who made the whole venture possible.

TABLE OF CONTENTS

According to information provided by the Library of Congress copyright office, the poem HIGH FLIGHT by John Gillespie Magee, Jr. was published in the "New York Herald Tribune", February 8, 1942. The facts of record for this issue are as follows:

NEW YORK HERALD TRIBUNE; Vol. 101, No. 34783, February 6, 1942. Registered in the name of New York Tribune, Inc., B 529721 following publication February 8, 1942.

No renewal was found for the periodical or the contribution.

PROLOGUE

Summer 1995. There were only a few houses on twenty-six acre Niskey Lake, when Dick and I built our stucco home nearly fifty years ago about thirty-five feet from the water's edge, an exciting forty-five degree slope down from the street. From the screened porch, I looked across the peaceful cove at the neighboring houses. They varied from modest to the pricey home of the doctor. At first, it was mostly white in this popular community on the south side of Atlanta. Now it's mostly black; only three other white families remain. I get along with my neighbors and go to the community gatherings. It's a lovely area with a beautiful tree-lined road around the lake and my home is so much a part of me, when the time comes to move on, I know I'll leave a part of my being in my house by the water.

A wild duck flew past breaking the late morning silence with its gravely call complaining about the mid-June heat. I looked around the porch, wiping beads of perspiration from my face. The metal chairs have held up well and I would have enjoyed stretching out for a few minutes on one of the comfortable old wrought-iron twin recliners where Dick and I used to relax and watch the baseball games on a small portable TV. It was too hot. The porch looked pretty good; the lake didn't. It's smooth glassy surface reflected the surrounding trees and lush green growth, but it hurt to see it clogged with algae and strange, clouded water plant life. I remember when it was clear as a bell and the happy late afternoons when I swam across and back before dinner.

We've had two cars in the lake. Both occasions sparked considerable activity, first from me and then from Dick. The first time was when Dick parked and forgot to put on the brakes. After dark, I heard an unusual sound, looked outside and saw Dick's car gently slide into the water. I got terribly excited and shouted for Dick to come look at the strange sight. The car had submerged with its lights on looking for all the world like some weird water vehicle out of the mind of Jules Verne. Dick wandered onto the porch, took one look and declared it was not a dreadful emergency after all. I said, "But, Dick, the lights are on!" His response was: "Don't worry, Birdie. It's not going anywhere. I'll call a tow truck in the morning." He drove it to the airport the next night.

Dick was the most unflappable man I've ever known, but when the second car took a dip, he reacted with his adrenaline in full gear, but not his brains. This happened one night when I was a nurse on the three to eleven shift at Piedmont Hospital and a beautiful young neighbor had offered to drive by to bring some medicine for Dick's parents, who lived with us. Full of youthful vigor and enthusiasm over her mission of mercy, she made a rapid, confident descent down our steep drive, continued into the lake and began to sink. Dick, who was undressed and ready to retire, heard her screams and got so excited, he put on a brand new pair of slacks I had just bought for him and jumped into the water to rescue the girl. Shortly thereafter, we built a two-foot high brick retainer wall. It's holding its own very well and anything else which comes its way. More than one person has expressed appreciation.

The paddle boat, down by the dock, is still a popular means of transportation for all the friends and kinfolk who come to visit. The old canoe is gone, though the memories remain of the many evenings Dick and I used to go fishing til eleven o'clock in order to have some privacy from his parents.

I walked back into the empty house and looked around at the clutter. I have my own type of filing system, which means the place is filled with papers, pictures and memorabilia on every table, in every nook and cranny; memories of family, my childhood, nursing, flying with Delta, Dick's flying with Eastern, the many organizations we belonged to, out friends, the war, and all the years Dick and I lived here, sometimes fussing, but most of the time enjoying each other, always on the go, draining every drop of good times from the life we shared.

I thought about a recent talk I had given at the Airport Marriott at a Delta luncheon for its flight attendants. It was quite a gathering. All the flight attendants who had ever flown with Delta were invited. Approximately a hundred and fifty showed up from near and far; fresh-faced young girls, older active attendants and retirees. I started recalling the early days of Delta, when I was one of the ten original stewardesses, the one chosen to go on the inaugural flight from Atlanta to Fort Worth, becoming Delta's first "in-air" stewardess by a crazy, mechanical fluke. I told one story after another to an enthusiastic audience and when the program was over, a number of the young girls crowded around and said, "You ought to write a book about your experiences, so everyone can know what it was like "back then", having to be a registered nurse in order to be a stewardess, living through World War Two and all the things that happened so long ago." I smiled and said, "I'm going to do just that."

This was a repeat performance of requests made by many people throughout the country, through the years to put my experiences on paper and share a part of my life: growing up in Vernon, Alabama, the tribulations and rewards of being a nurse in the 1930's, the continuing joyride of marriage with Dick, and what it was like in the practically prehistoric period of early commercial flight.

This book is in response to those countless requests. The first chapters provide a glimpse of my early years, but the main body of the book is devoted to the time I left home in 1933 to become a nurse; my time with Delta, including the exciting inaugural flight of Delta's stewardess service; my courtship with Dick, our unusual double wedding; his war injury during the invasion of Sicily, and our ultimate return to civilian life in 1945.

May those who have survived this former time zone enjoy the memories. May the younger generation join in the laughter and tears as they learn about a by-gone era.

PART ONE

Birdie Bomar & Kathryn Bankston

Chapter 1

A CHRISTMAS GIFT…ME!

From the very beginning I knew I was meant to fly. Even my name reflected my destiny. On the day I was born, Mama, God rest her soul, named me Birdie and ever since I can remember, people have asked me about it and since you're taking your time to read my story, at the outset I'd like to tell you how Mama pulled it off.

Day one for me began about three o'clock in the morning a couple of days before Christmas 1913. Mama always said I was the nicest Christmas present she ever had. Daddy was also happy to have me. He just wished I'd decided to come at a more convenient hour. Mama didn't have to make a long trip to the hospital in the middle of the night because I was born at home, so everything was fine with her. One time was just as good as another. Things were different for Daddy. He had to go get the doctor and he couldn't just hop on the back of the horse. He had to hitch up the cart, so he'd be able to bring the doctor back with him, that is if the doctor was functioning. Daddy knew the shady side of Doc Graham (not his real name) and said a quick prayer.

Back then, practically nobody went to the hospital to have a baby. Hospitals weren't popular. People were afraid of them. Naturally, if you were real bad off, a hospital was good to have around; the closer the better.

Our small farm house was not close by. It was over a hundred miles from the nearest hospital in Birmingham, so if anything had gone wrong; if I had hesitated about being born, if Mama had problems, my life might have been entirely different. It might not even have gotten started. As it was, things went along as well as could be expected, except that Daddy's worst fears came to pass. The doctor had backslid. Here's the way Daddy used to tell it.

He always talked about how brave Mama was. For several hours, she put up with me creating a ruckus wanting to come out to see the Christmas tree and after having enough of my disturbance, she reached over and nudged him and said, "John Wesley, get Doc Graham. The baby's coming."

Daddy got all worked up. He bundled up quick as a flash, leaned over and gave Mama a quick peck on the cheek and said, "Hold on, Clara. I'll be back as soon as I can."

It was close to midnight when Daddy drove out of the barn to bring back Doc Graham to deliver his first born. Daddy rode hard and fast about a mile down the unpaved road. There was a bright moon to show the way and Daddy always said God had the sky all lighted up with His own Christmas decorations, with a million stars sparkling for this special occasion.

He pulled up to Doc Graham's large frame house. Everything was quiet and closed up. He knocked on the door and waited for signs of life. The air was crisp and cold. He knocked again and rubbed his hands together to keep warm. Inside a front window, he saw a light approaching. The door opened a crack and Mrs. Graham shone the lantern in his face.

"Mrs. Graham, Clara's time has come. She needs Doc right away. I brought my cart to take him."

Mrs. Graham pulled her old faded pink chenille robe around her, pushed back her gray pigtail and opened the door. "Come on in, John. Doctor Graham is a little under the weather. Have a seat and I'll see if he can make it." Mrs. Graham lit a candle in the parlor and disappeared down the hall. Daddy said he was too excited too sit. He just paced up and down as he heard Mrs. Graham trying to rouse her husband. He also heard a thick-tongued response and his heart sank. He thought, "My God! Doc Graham's drunk!"

Everybody knew Doc had been backsliding and the season must have spurred him to spread a little more Christmas cheer than he could handle. Mrs. Graham hurried back into the front room, with the solid, patient acceptance that made everybody respect her.

"I'm sorry, John. Doctor Graham can't go, but there's a new young doctor who's just moved in down the road about five minutes from here. Doctor Duncan's his name (not his real name). Look for his name on the mailbox. God bless you and Clara. Tell Clara I'll drop by in the morning."

Back home, Daddy did some more pacing outside the room where I was due and when the time was right, I cooperated. Mama cooperated. The sober young substitute doctor did his thing with nobody to help him except for Daddy bringing in big pails of hot water, and suddenly I was there yelling to high heaven to let the world know I had arrived. Daddy was nervous and excited like most young fathers and to him, the whole experience was a miracle. When he came in, Doctor Duncan had me all bundled up sweet and clean as could be and in my adult opinion, I'm sure I looked like a cherub; a rather red cherub.

For my worldly debut, God gave me a mop of flaming red hair just like Mama and Daddy, and that was nice. I was also kind of red all over from the exertion of getting born and I let out vehement protests at some of the indignities of the process. Like most mothers who are blind to the imperfections of their children, Mama smiled and proudly displayed me to Daddy. "Isn't she beautiful!"

Daddy tried hard to conceal his mixed emotions. He cleared his throat with a grunt, bent over to get a better look and said, "She sure is red."

I expect Daddy had been secretly hoping for a son, but he tried to be nice about it since there wasn't much to be done about it at that point. He pulled up a chair and sat down by the bed. Well,

Clara, what do you want to name our new daughter?"

Daddy hadn't volunteered any girl names and Mama had kept quiet on the subject, but now it came out.

"Birdie."

"Birdie?"

The words came quietly from Mama's lips. "For an artist in Birmingham. She paints the most beautiful birds."

Now Daddy came from a very conservative background. He was used to girl names like Mary Jane, Elizabeth, Dorothy Sue, maybe even Victoria and Prudence. On the inside he probably thought, "Good grief!" On the outside, he didn't let it show. He just sat there and mulled it over for a long minute, came to the conclusion it could have been worse and gave in. Daddy always tried to be a gentleman.

"Well, I reckon that's good enough reason. She's a bird all right. A pretty little red bird." he said with growing enchantment about his new role in life.

"Yessiree, she's a real bird all right. And I'll bet she's gonna do some high flying in her day!"

And that's the way it was.

Chapter 2

GROWING UP IN VERNON, POPULATION 700

Harry Truman once said he didn't have any regard for people who put on false airs and pretended they came from some sophisticated metropolitan area when they really came from a two-horse town. He felt that a hometown was part of a person and he had no use for anybody who couldn't own up to his background. President Truman was born in a small town; Lamar, Missouri. I can't even claim to have been born in a small town. I was born out in the countryside, but I did most of my growing up in a small community and I'm still proud of where I came from and cherish the memories I have of Vernon, Alabama.

The heart of Vernon was dominated by the courthouse in the middle of the square, like it is in so many small towns across America. It was an old brick Greek revival building with four impressive white columns in front, crested with a white wood steeple, complete with pigeons, which the current mayor tried to get rid of and failed. The businesses needed to keep a community going occupied the store space on the street surrounding the courthouse and massive gnarled oaks intertwined their leafy branches out into the street, creating a shady sanctuary on hot summer days and a scene of beauty with their changing color in the Fall. I even liked to look at them in their wintertime skeletal bareness, knowing they would come to life again in the Spring. To me, they were symbols of strength, stability and immortality.

The courthouse had a low cement wall that went all the way around it. It was popular with anybody who wanted to sit and rest a spell, particularly the older men, who would park on the little wall-seat talking with each other or listening to an inspired itinerant preacher give vent to his feelings, warning the good folk about hell-fire and damnation for the sinners and a heavenly reward awaiting the faithful. There were four cement walks leading up to the four entrances to the courthouse. These were the greatest places in town to roller skate, especially on chilly fall days after school when chores had been attended to. Skinned knees, bruises and all.

During the week, people came and went in moderate numbers, but on Saturday the great immigration began early in the morning and the downtown section of Vernon hummed with the activity of folks from the immediate area and outlying farms. According to the weather, they drove their horse and buggies over rough, dry, dusty roads or wet muddy ones with holes filled with dirty mud-red water. And as the years went by, the paved streets expanded and the priviledged few who owned automobiles continued to grow, Saturday was still "shopping" day, the day to stock up on provisions. It was the day to go to the barbershop when absolutely necessary and Vernon had two. Somehow, it seems like people were a little friendlier then. Most everybody smiled and greeted one another and it was a good feeling.

The movie house opened when I was a senior in high school. It was an immediate success. Everybody, young and old alike, went to be entertained whenever time and budget allowed.

There were a few older citizens who felt the whole town was going to hell, but Saturday afternoon, the theatre was crammed with boisterous folks who were lucky enough to have finished their tasks and had a dime to get in. The standard Saturday fare included a full-length movie, a newsreel to keep us up with what was going on in the world, even though it was usually a few days old, and the weekly serial, which was just as important as the main feature. It always left you sitting on the edge of your seat with a life-threatening challenge for the hero, and for seven days, you had to wait for the next episode to find out what happened, and if you didn't get your tasks done, or some other disaster occurred to keep you from going, it was a keen disappointment.

The movie house was on one corner of the town square. On another, the respected Bank of Vernon occupied a handsome brick building, displaying the architectural ingenuity of the time. It was designed to face the corner, with rounded windows at the top on one side and regular oblong windows on the other. This is the bank where Daddy borrowed the money for me to go to nursing school. As a public relations gesture, Mr. Jones, the owner, had wooden shelves built inside the sun-filled windows for the townswomen to put their houseplants during the winter and it was nice to see the greenery, when the rest of the world was bare.

In addition to the Yellow Front Store, which really had a yellow front, there were a number of businesses including: Courier Printing, the offices of the Lamar Democrat, the town newspaper, and the Telephone Office, which played a vital role in providing communications, because hardly anyone had a phone at home. The City Hall and the Police Department were in the courthouse. There was also the drugstore, where everybody met and had the best milk shakes in the world. Grady Roberts, the owner-pharmacist. was kind about letting the young folks hang around and look at magazines they didn't buy, because he knew the young folks had probably blown the last of their weekly budget on one of his fine milk shakes.

Vernon was big enough to accommodate two general stores, but it was a hassle for the second one to compete with the older established Yellow Front Store. To lure business in his direction, the second store owner set up a pool table in the rear of the building, so you had to pass by all the tempting merchandise. It was an acceptable place for recreation, where high school students stopped by after school.

Vernon was the only town in the county not on a main artery of transportation. People were drawn to it because it was in the center of the county and was the designated home of the county courthouse. They were more or less compelled to come to Vernon. They came for different types of legal documents, which had to be filed in the courthouse. They came to settle differences of opinion in court and sometimes to prosecute criminals. In earlier days, it was a hearty frontier town. Lamar County was rich in Indian history and many an evening, I heard tales of the past at the parental knee.

The Paleo Indians were the aboriginal tribe going back thousands of years. Later on, the Chickasaws and Choctaws came because of the rich supply of fish and game. They fished, bathed and washed their clothes in the Luxapallila River, which means "Turtle There Crawls Creek" and the last time I looked, it still gave sanctuary to those slow-moving creatures of ancient heritage. The Indians elevated their standard of living by building houses and teaching their young braves to defend their land. Evidence of the hunting and warfare could still be found back in the 1930's in a rich deposit of arrowheads. My sister, Lema, didn't care much about them, but my brother,

Elvin, and I had a nice collection of these primitive chiseled stones.

The Indians have been long gone, although occasionally, you ran into part-Indians, and probably still do. When I lived in Vernon, there was a Mr. Brown Bear, who lived out from the town on a small farm. I always felt a kindred soul with the Indians, because Mama told me proudly that I had a small amount of Cherokee blood coursing through my veins. I'm not quite sure where or when this occurred, but I was told that it was supposed to help make me physically strong.

Chapter 3
THE ACCEPTANCE LETTER

Going to church was a required activity in our home. That didn't mean you were going to listen to the sermon, but there was one time, the preacher caught my ear. He started talking about how things can change in the twinkling of an eye and in a poor Alabama farming community during the great depression era, it was a much needed reminder. This biblical message actually pertains to victory over physical death, but the preacher said there were many types of resurrection like turning from fear to faith, hate to love, resentment to forgiveness and despair to hope. I remember him talking about how something could happen in a flash and from then on your life would never be the same. He said it's one of life's great mysteries; what makes life exciting and gives us hope. I took all that twinkling to mean something good. That's what I counted on and so far as I was concerned, on that hot summer Sunday, the preacher hit a homer for sure.

At this time, in Vernon, Alabama some seven hundred souls worked and strived for a living from the soil or offered goods and services through individual small businesses. Without one of those God-given "twinkles" there wasn't much chance of becoming rich or famous, much less finding a husband unless you were mighty easily pleased, or lucky, or plain conniving. Everybody knew everybody else in town, so you knew what your chances were and mine didn't look so good to me. Still I left the house one morning a few days after that fine sermon with hope in my heart, remembering the preacher had said that hope, love and faith were the beginning of most of life's miracles.

It was late summer, the year I was nineteen, and every day I'd been looking for a letter from Birmingham and every day brought the time closer when the news would have to come, whether it was good or bad.

Everything seemed so routine on that particular morning. It was quiet and peaceful as I left home to get the mail from the post office. It was about ten o'clock and the thermometer on the back porch had already hit over eighty and I knew it was going to be a scorcher.

As I walked along, I greeted all the neighbors who were outside. They saw me making my daily pilgrimage and knew how anxious I was. With Mama's wise encouragement, I had applied at South Highland Infirmary to enter its nursing school. And every day I waited. And hoped.

Word of mouth was the fastest means of communication in Lamar County at that time. Most folks didn't have a telephone, but news got around. News about people coming and going. Getting born or dying. Courting. Getting Married. Or not getting married: especially if somebody got jilted. The news got around about the mines. The crops. The church activities. The depression.

It was almost four years since the stock market collapsed and caused a lot of heartache. All of a sudden, there wasn't any money going around and you wondered what had happened to it. We surely weren't a rich community, but we were used to having things a lot easier and when the money vanished, it was hard to take. You heard stories about unemployment, hungry families, the long bread lines and occasionally, stories about men jumping out of tall buildings in the big cities. I'm grateful Daddy wasn't one of them. He did all kinds of work to keep us going. Mama's job at the Yellow Front Store brought home forty dollars a month and all the children pitched in and helped with the household chores.

Before the depression, I was just a little girl, but I remember the good life we had. We weren't rich, but we had all we needed.

Our home in Vernon was a large frame house, with a half-moon concrete driveway in front and beautiful old magnolias that smelled sweet as could be when the huge white blossoms opened in the late spring. We had a garden in back with vegetables which provided food for the body and flowers which gave us colorful food for the soul. The outhouse was also in back; way back. I never knew the joys of indoor plumbing until after I went off to nursing school.

The main house was painted a dark green trimmed in white. It had a big porch that wrapped around the front and one side. When you entered the front door, you walked right into the living room on the right side, through lovely French doors to the dining room, then to the kitchen, which led to the large, screened-in back porch, where there was generally a lot of activity. Daddy put the pump from the well there, so we didn't have to go out to draw water like a lot of people. The back porch also had an icebox with a separate compartment for the ice, delivered in twenty-five and fifty-pound blocks, hauled in on large tongs by the iceman. That's where Mama made sauerkraut from cabbage fresh from the garden. That's where she canned and preserved fresh fruits and vegetables. As I grew up, I learned to do these things, and despite the depression years, we generally had plenty of good eating.

On the left side of the house, there were three bedrooms and when the family got indoor plumbing, after I had left home, the front room which had been mine had a closet, which Daddy converted into a bathroom with a door opening into the hall so everybody had access to it. Indoor plumbing did away with all the activities on the back porch and this area was made into a fourth bedroom. The far-sighted builder had put a bathroom adjacent to the back porch, but for about ten years it couldn't be used as such, because Vernon had neither water nor sewage. When the happy day arrived, my family was fortunate to have not one, but two bathrooms and in those days, that was pure luxury for anyone living in Vernon. I wish I might have been around to enjoy them.

The miracles of modern technology were slow in coming to our home. I suppose the most marvelous one to arrive before I left home was the Delco system. Daddy installed this amazing piece of equipment in a small dark green wooden house in the back yard. And, oh, the joy and excitement! The whole neighborhood came to watch the progress and completion of the installation and the shelter to protect it. The Delco system meant that we could enter the world of the privileged, who enjoyed electricity in their homes. It meant no more reading and studying by an Aladin lamp; no more groping in a dark closet for clothes and things; no more anxious moments about getting your makeup on straight, or leaving home with mismated shoes, no more worry about engaging in any of the activities that are made easier by being able to see what you're doing, like sewing, or cooking, or playing the piano.

We shared our Delco system with a neighbor a couple of doors down the street. This helped to cut down on the expense and the maintenance because it seems Daddy and the neighbor were always working on it. I remember it was just a few months before I graduated from high school. It was about dusk when Daddy shouted happily, "Let there be light!" And the one 60-watt light bulb dangling from a cord in the center of the ceiling in the living room poured its brightness on a small, enthusiastic gathering.

Lest we should get carried away with our new luxury, Daddy hurried into the house and gave us instructions about its usage. The system would run only from about three or four in the afternoon til bedtime at ten o'clock and under no circumstances were we to fool around with the equipment. The womenfolk could have cared less, but the restriction was hard on my brother Elvin, who liked to tinker with mechanical things.

After the excitement of getting electricity, we got a radio. Mother and Daddy (that meant Daddy) decided what programs were listened to and none of the children were to turn it on without parental permission. I don't remember ever paying much attention to this newfangled gadget, but Daddy got a lot of pleasure out of listening to the news and the prize fights.

Our family never had a telephone in the house as long as I lived there. Most folks today would be lost without this means of communication, but we survived very well. With no phone, no television or loud stereo sets, and limited use of the new radio, life was a lot more peaceful. We didn't feel deprived. We had all the socializing we needed or wanted and I always had lots of friends.

I graduated with thirty-seven of them from Lamar County High School. We were all filled with high hopes, despite the depressed economy and most of the class wanted to go to college. I was one of those, but all my hoping didn't make it happen. Daddy couldn't afford to send me to college, and it hurt. Especially since a lot of my friends were going. Some were going to Mississippi State. A couple were heading for Auburn and several were going to the University of Alabama. That's where I really wanted to go, but there was no way I could do it and I was determined not to stay in a small Alabama town, where there was no opportunity to do anything except clerk in one of the local stores, be a waitress, or sell tickets at the movie house. I don't mean to put down these kinds of jobs. My wonderful Mama worked at the Yellow Front Store. I worked in some of these places myself. I simply knew this wasn't the way I wanted to spend the rest of my life, especially since there weren't all that many eligible men around.

There was some talk about me going to Livingston State Teachers College in south

Alabama. I would have had to work as a waitress in the school cafeteria to help pay my tuition and would have lived with a family out in the country. This kind of turned my stomach. I didn't really want to be a teacher even though that's what Daddy wanted me to do and I knew I didn't want to live with some strange family way out in the jumping off place. It had now been a year since I graduated from high school. And I knew something had to be done to get on with my life.

I didn't know it when I started to the post office that day, but that something was just about to happen. This was getting ready to turn into one of the most important days of my life.

The tree-shaded sidewalk gave way to the town's business district, which was never very busy during the week and this morning, the intense heat had discouraged all but the most determined shoppers. The door to the post office was open to catch whatever breeze might come its way. My neighbor, Mr. Johnson, the tall, lean postmaster, was red-faced from the heat. He had his shirtsleeves rolled up and his green celluloid visor tilted back on his head. There was a small, metal rotating table fan purring away on the counter. It tried, but it didn't do much good.

Mr. Johnson was sorting mail that had arrived by truck from Sulligent, eleven miles away, where the train passed through. He looked up.

"There's a letter in your box I think you've been waiting for," he said matter of factly.

With a feeling of mounting excitement, I hurried to our box and my mind and my fingers had a hard time coordinating the simple combination lock. After a couple of fumbles, which seemed an eternity, the lock popped open and I pulled out the one piece of mail in the compartment. A quick glance at the return address confirmed the fact.

This was it!

My heart raced so hard, it just about jumped out of my body and I felt I had to run to keep up with it.

I dashed by Mr. Johnson, who looked like nothing at all had happened and was half way down the block when I stopped to open the envelope. I read the brief message, let out a joyous whoop and started jumping up and down and spinning around. A couple of elderly women passed by and saw my antics, but I didn't care. I didn't care either when I heard one of them say; "I wonder what's happened to the Perkins girl? She's always been unpredictable."

I was no longer walking. I was floating. My feet barely touched the ground as I bounded home.

I hurried along, passing out the glad tidings to everyone I saw. I felt like a pony express rider carrying a message of such magnitude as to change the whole structure of society in Vernon, Alabama. After all, I was leaving. I was going to be a nurse and take care of people and help them get well. I was going to help them live and be happy. I was going to be the next Florence Nightingale! And I wanted everybody to share my joy.

Chapter 4

BE PREPARED AND TRUST IN THE LORD

Mama was swinging quietly on the front porch shelling peas for dinner, when I came running up the sidewalk. "It's come! It's come, Mama!" I shouted, taking the front porch steps two at a time. Despite the heat, Mama looked cool and crisp in her pink floral cotton dress. She was a pretty woman who had the knack of taking almost everything in her stride. She pushed back a strand of her rich auburn hair and cautioned, "Birdie, calm down before you have a heart attack." My younger brother and sister barged through the screen door to see what all the commotion was about.

Mama took charge. "Everybody sit down and let's hear Birdie's letter." My redheaded baby sister, Lema, sat beside Mama on the swing. My redheaded blue-jeaned teenage brother, Elvin, plopped on the floor, while I sat in Daddy's favorite wooden rocker and read aloud.

"Dear Miss Perkins:" I was so worked up, I felt like I had no breath. "Due to a last minute cancellation, a position has become available in our next nurses training program." Mama interrupted, "Slow down, Birdie."

"Classes will start Monday, August 21st, therefore it is necessary that you report here by 6 P.M., Friday, August 18th in time for the orientation sessions starting Saturday morning at 8 A.M."

Elvin broke in. "Hey! That's today! You've got to be there by six o'clock tonight!"

I continued, "If you are not here by the 18th, you will forfeit this opportunity and won't be eligible for admission until the class which starts next year. I regret this last minute notice, but I hope you may be able to join us for this session. Sincerely, Augusta Ann Smith, Director of Nurses Training, South Highland Infirmary."

Mama rose from the swing and started giving out directions as she headed for the kitchen with the shelled peas. "Elvin, go up in the attic and bring down the big black suitcase. Birdie; go pick out the clothes you want to take with you. Lema, see what you can do to help your sister." Elvin broke in, "How's she gonna get there?" Mama ignored the question and continued, "Birdie, bring me that pretty beige cotton suit I made for you last week. I'll press it and you can wear it with your orange blouse. That should make a good impression on the city folks."

From that moment on, the mad pace to get ready accelerated til I felt like a character out of those old-timey movies where the film is jerky and runs too fast. Clothes started flying through the air. There was a lot of loud discussion about what all could get into one suitcase and all the hullabaloo didn't let up til Daddy came home for dinner around noon.

It was crazy. Here I was, supposed to be in Birmingham by six o'clock. There were no trains. No busses operating out of Vernon and I didn't know how I was going to get there. I just knew it. "Daddy will find a way." Mama knew it. "The Lord will provide." And now Daddy was going to know about it, with the whole burden thrown on his shoulders. He had just come inside and was taking off his straw hat, displaying the standard crop of Perkins red hair and was putting his hat on top of the coat rack when I ran to meet him.

"Daddy, my acceptance has come! I'm leaving to go to South Highland Infirmary!" I said joyfully.

Daddy was not joyful about the information. He had never been happy about my going to be a nurse. He didn't like it at all and made no secret about his feelings. I think he felt like I was hitting very close to walking the primrose path. So when I told him I was leaving, he didn't say anything. He just grunted like he did more than usual, since the depression set in. He walked across the living room and sat in his favorite chair, a well-worn recliner, which seemed almost molded to his medium frame. He looked at me with his clear blue eyes.

"When're you leaving, Sport?"

I blurted out, "I have to be there by six.

"That's six o'clock tomorrow? Next week?"

"No, sir. I have to be there by six this evening, or I'll miss out."

"Have you given any thought about how you're going to get there?"

"No, sir. I thought you'd know what to do." I guess I was like most young folks who feel like their parents can master any situation.

"You realize it's a hundred and ten miles to Birmingham. It's already after twelve and it's going to take a good four hours to get there?"

"Yes, sir. I thought maybe you might know somebody who might know somebody going in that direction. People are coming and going all the time."

Daddy just sat there staring off into space, not saying anything for a few minutes. He just sat there and stared and rubbed his chin. Mama was coming in from the kitchen, when Daddy got up. He looked tired.

"Hold dinner for a while, Clara. I'll be back in half an hour."

Daddy knew I was depending on him and he reacted like most fathers, who are emotionally torn about what they think is best for their children; sometimes feeling heartsick and guilty because they don't have enough money to make life easier for them. Daddy also realized that I was grown, with a mind of my own. And being of his own begetting, he knew my head was made of something close to the consistency of solid rock. He knew when I made up my mind to do something, I didn't stop until I had accomplished my goal. And he was determined to help the best way he knew how, even if he did think Mama and I were scatterbrained to start packing before we knew a way to get there.

He entered the local bank and went straight to the president's office. The door was open and Sherrill Jones beckoned him to come in.

Daddy got a loan for twenty-five dollars to cover my expenses for the training period. Mr. Jones was used to listening to much more desperate appeals for money and this was taken care of in short order. He even arranged a ride to Birmingham for me. Mr. Jones was a true friend.

Sam Dawson (not his real name) was my delegated chaffeur. He was a pharmaceutical salesman who was leaving that afternoon to go back to Birmingham. Mr. Jones assured Daddy, "I've known Sam close to ten years. He's dependable as the day's long. He'll take good care of your little girl. Tell Birdie to be ready by two. Sam will be there."

When I saw Daddy walk back into the house, his whole appearance showed he'd met with success. He wasn't happy, but there was an air of confidence and satisfaction that he had done his paternal duty. He had managed a crisis for his firstborn and was resigned to the fact that I was leaving.

While we were eating midday dinner, Daddy told us about the arrangements he'd made. Mama was accepting. She trusted Mr. Jones' judgement. She was also understanding about my going to nursing school. She knew there weren't any opportunities in Vernon for a young woman without a college education. Even with a degree there wasn't much a woman could do other than teach. Mama had always encouraged me to give nursing a try. She used to talk about how she admired the English nurse, Florence Nightingale, who had won the hearts of people all over the world. Mama always had high hopes for her children. She believed the Lord would provide and that we'd amount to something somehow.

The sun was sparkling outside. It wasn't sparkling on the inside. All of us were going through the painful process of trying not to show our emotions. We were generally a talkative family, always sharing our thoughts and experiences, but conversation reached an all-time low, while we were each wrapped up in our own feelings. We always leaned on one other for an often unspoken love and had a strong sense of loyalty, which magnified the joy of living our lives together. I knew my leaving would create a vacuum and a heartache that would take a while to heal; even for Daddy, who always seemed so strong. And I just couldn't let myself think about how much I was going to miss my family. Daddy made a stab at conversation.

"Sport, there are lots of bad things that can happen in a big city and I want you to be careful about the people you associate with."

Mama admonished me to establish a church contact. "Just because you're going to be away from the influence of your parents, I don't want you to neglect the Lord. Besides, going to church is a good way to meet respectable people." Most of the time, Mama was practical.

I responded with "yes, mams" and "yes, sirs" as I picked at my food. And as the hands of the wall clock approached two, I became quieter and quieter. I felt like a robot as I slipped into my new beige suit. It must have been ninety degrees. I was sweating, but I felt like I had ice water in my veins and my stomach didn't feel too confident. By the time Mr. Dawson drove up to the front door, all my enthusiasm and worldly ambition had vanished and I began to feel like a sacrificial lamb headed for slaughter.

"Elvin yelled, "Birdie! That man's here!"

Mr. Dawson rang the door bell. Daddy welcomed him into the living room and I could hear his cordial greeting. "Come in, Sam. I'm John Perkins. This is my wife Clara and this is little Lema and Elvin." He called to me. "Come on, Birdie. Mr. Dawson's here."

Mr. Dawson reassured Mama and Daddy. "Don't you worry about Miss Birdie. I'll take good care of her and personally turn her over to the lady in charge. But there's no time to waste. We need to get going." With the finality of those words, suddenly I felt like all of this wasn't really happening. But it was.

Lots of hugs and kisses were exchanged and it was worse than a funeral. With a funeral, at least the departed doesn't complicate matters by crying and carrying on. But I was very much alive, with strong feelings and a strong attachment to my family. I had never spent a night away from home, except an occasional visit at grandmother's and it was hard to keep back the tears.

Lema clung to Mama and sobbed openly. She had just lost her pet dog in an automobile accident and with my leaving, a major part of her small world was collapsing. Elvin was now fifteen and felt almost grown, so he just kicked the dirt around and pretended to wipe the perspiration off on his shirtsleeve. Mama held up better than any of us. Mothers are like that sometimes, most of the time, when they know they have to be strong. She gave me a small bag of fruit. "You're going to be just fine, Birdie."

Daddy had the final word. "You take good care of your-self, Sport."

Mama dabbed a speck in her eye. Daddy grunted a little more than usual and blew his nose. And finally, we were on the road.

Chapter 5

THE JOURNEY TO BIRMINGHAM

It didn't take long to get on the main road. You could get anywhere in town in five minutes unless you had a flat tire or some obstacle blocked your path. It was three-quarters of a mile from home to the highway and when we reached the open road, it hit me. I thought, "Here I am sitting next to a man I've never seen before and I'm going to be sitting next to him for the next four hours." I was trapped. I was scared. And it was hot. Real hot. It must have been a hundred degrees and the metal bucket Mr. Dawson had filled with a fifty-pound block of ice and placed between us didn't do much good.

I looked out at the green cotton fields passing by. I knew they'd soon be turning fluffy and white and I knew I wouldn't be around to see them and a sense of nostalgia swept over me that left my heart aching for the life I was leaving behind. I had been dry-eyed for about ten or fifteen minutes and now the tears rushed out like water through a broken dam. There didn't seem to be anything I could do to stem the tide and the delicate little hanky Mama had given me just before leaving wasn't equal to my performance.

Mr. Dawson seemed to be a kindly man with a good face, but I thought he was so old. He must have been forty-five or fifty, with soft grey eyes and thin brown hair turning grey at the temples. He knew I was miserable and he began to look very uncomfortable. He shifted his weight a lot and I guess he was trying his best to pretend this wasn't happening, but as my crying became more vocal, he reached in his pocket and pulled out a fresh, white man-size handkerchief. He handed it to me and said, "Try this one, missy."

Life at that moment seemed unreal and painful. I remembered Daddy's comforting words, "Anytime you want to leave the infirmary, Sport, I'll come get you." He had even threatened to do it whether I wanted to leave or not. He was upset about my going to be a nurse. One day, I overheard him talking to Mama about rumors he'd heard about hospitals having a bad reputation, especially in their training programs for nurses. He'd heard disturbing stories about the long working hours, the physically demanding labor and the humiliation many young women were subjected to. But, he didn't try to stop me. I guess Mama won out on that argument. He and Mama had always taught me to believe in myself. They said, "If you make up your mind there's something you want to do and if you work hard enough, you should be able to accomplish your goal." And I discovered that sometimes, it didn't require as much work as you thought it would; sometimes just getting started and having the determination that you would succeed could help you do it.

Thinking about the challenge ahead helped to dry the tears for a while and I drifted off into a period of quiet reverie. The heat and the soft drone of the motor lulled me and I don't how long I dozed, until we went over a rough stretch of dirt road and I came back to the present.

I looked at Mr. Dawson. He was flushed from the heat. He broke the silence.

"How'd you like a cold drink, Miss Birdie? I'm going to need some gas and we should be coming to a good stopping place soon. We can fill up the car and stretch our legs a bit."

A couple of miles on down the road, small frame houses started getting closer together. We could see chickens scratching around in the yards and an occasional horse, or cow, or goat and a few minutes later; a roadside station came into view. The wooden structure didn't look too sturdy, but there were a couple of gas pumps and a rusty cold drink sign to let us know our needs could be met.

Mr. Dawson bought me an orange crush and some crackers filled with peanut butter. I stood around, while he and the station owner talked about the drought and how it was going to hurt the economy. There was a loud hum in the sky and we all looked up to see a small two-seater plane with an open cockpit. Mr. Dawson spoke with authority, "That pilot's been out dusting crops close by." The owner of the facility agreed. "Yep. I seen 'em 'round these parts a lot lately. This here barn-storming is gettin' real poplar."

Mr. Dawson nodded his head. "Looks like it might be a great way to make a living. The way he's cavorting around up there looks like he's having a good time."

"Yep. My nephew tole me bout goin' up in one of them planes over in Birmin'ham. He said these here pilots go round to different towns and take people up for a joy ride." He rubbed the stubble of his beard; turned his head, thank goodness, and spat out the longest squirt of tobacco juice I'd ever seen. "Myself, I feel like if the Lord had intended me to fly, he'd a given me wings. I think I'd ruther keep my feet on the ground."

Nobody bothered to ask me my opinion about the pilot or flying, but somewhere deep inside, I knew I'd go up in a plane some day and as I looked at that plane, I was sure I could fly one as good as anybody. I could just imagine the thrill of being a great stunt pilot, flying upside down, doing crazy loop-t-loops and all the rest of those strange, exotic, daring, wonderful maneuvers. But, nobody asked my thoughts on the subject.

Mr. Dawson paid the bill and we hit the road again on our hot debilitating journey.

I sat without talking, looking at the Alabama countryside: field after field of cotton, parched and reddish from the dust of the road; widely separated farm houses, sheltered by large oak trees, some with people sitting, rocking on the front porch, friendy folks who waved as we passed by. I looked at the homes with carefully tended gardens and neglected ones that made you know the owners had run into hard times. Most of the houses had animals in the yard: chickens, sometimes guinea hens, scratching around for food; an occasional rooster strutting by, proudly aware of his fine plumage; skinny hounddogs lying in the shade of a tree and cats, stretched out lazily on the porch, looking like they owned the place. Cows in the meadow hovering close to trees to escape the burning sun; horses and mules fenced by weather-worn bobbed wire, immobile, with only their tails in motion, brushing away the flies; animals the farmers depended on for their livelihood and kept too long behind the plow. The sun made its way down the western sky and the cake of ice had long since melted. Mr. Dawson broke the silence. "We'll stop soon for another block of ice. I figure we ought to get to Birmingham close to six and I'm sure if we're a few minutes late, they won't send you home."

I began to realize that this trip was just as hard on Mr. Dawson as it was on me and I tried to make an effort at conversation. I told him how I had wanted to be a basketball coach, how I had been driving a car since I was twelve years old and of the times I had run away from home in the family car and how one time Daddy had come to get me and several friends of mine who had made an impromptu trip to Birmingham. It was two o'clock in the morning. Daddy was pretty upset about the whole thing and starting the next evening, I had to write Proverbs 8:18 two hundred and fifty times. Fifty times per night Monday through Friday. I still remember the verse: He who walks in integrity will be delivered. But he who is perverse in his ways will fall into a pit.

My little excursion was in late Spring and car privileges were taken away til the end of the school year. I got a lot of exercise during the next two and a half months and my social life hit an all-time low.

By the time I finished my story, we were entering Birmingham. It wasn't a big city like New York or Chicago, but in comparison with Vernon, it was impressive and I wondered what it was going to be like living here. Mr. Dawson told me, "Our last child was born at South Highland. It's a good place, Miss Birdie. Has a fine reputation. You'll get good training so you can go anywhere you want to when you graduate. And you'll know you're well prepared."

As we drove into the parking area, I looked at the large brick building and steeled myself.

This was it. From now on, I was going to be on my own. I knew my life would never be the same again and I was determined to be brave and give it my best shot. The time for tears was over, although I felt queasy with excitement and resignation as Mr. Dawson carried my large, unsightly suitcase into the brightly lit lobby. It was an active, strange arena. There was a small group of people standing over to one side. A white-jacketed doctor was talking to them and an elderly woman was crying. A couple of nurses hurried by and I thought how efficient they looked, carrying little trays of medicine. A young man and his mother, I guess, were leaving, all full of smiles and he was saying excitedly, "I can't believe it! Twins!" And I knew how happy they must be.

We went to the information counter and asked for Miss Augusta Ann Smith. We were directed down the hall to a small office with Miss Smith's name on the door and underneath it: "Director of Nurses Training". I had met her once before when I first considered nursing, so I knew what to expect. She was a very attractive lady in her thirties. I thought she was pretty enough to be in the movies and as she spoke to us, she was so gracious, my stomach settled a little and I was sure I was going to make it.

After the usual words of introduction and greetings, she left the office for a few minutes and I turned to Mr. Dawson. "I'm sorry I broke down and I'm much obliged for the ride and the cold drink and crackers." Mr. Dawson looked at me in genuine compassion and I imagine he must have thought about his own daughter being in a situation like this. And I'm sure he was relieved to have completed his commitment.

He paid me a nice compliment. "You're a brave young lady, Miss Birdie, and I hope the rest of your life is going to be happier than it's been today. What you're doing takes a lot of courage and I wish you the very best." He raised his hand in a gesture of goodbye, walked back toward the lobby and as he disappeared around the corner, for the first time in my life, I felt totally alone, wondering what the future would hold.

Chapter 6

SOUTH HIGHLAND INFIRMARY

What the future held was dished out in small, but strong doses.

Miss Smith took me to a large dormitory room in the basement of the hospital. I was one of twelve girls who would start classes on Monday. Twelve small-size beds were lined up against one wall. A footlocker graced the end of each cot. On the opposite wall were twelve small closets. There were no frills to soften the Spartan accommodations, but I was pleased because I was going to be stepping up in the world. I was going to have indoor plumbing! The joy dimmed only slightly, when I found there was only one bathroom for twelve girls. I knew it was going to be a busy place, but at least we didn't have to go to an outhouse.

It was the dinner hour and the large, empty room seemed strange. Various suitcases and clothing were piled on most of the beds by girls, who had arrived too late to get things in order before eating. Miss Smith designated an empty cot for me. I placed my bulky, black grip on the bed and followed her to the dining room to meet my fellow students.

Classes started promptly at nine A.M. Monday. Most of them were held in large, unadorned classrooms, in a building, which would accommodate sixty nurses. The eager, youthful students were excited and nervous starting the demanding four months probationary period. As usual, I was sweating, but I was not alone. There was no air-conditioning and it was hot.

South Highland was known for its strict code of ethics and high scholastic standards. If you were caught cheating, there was no second chance. Immediately, you became past history. If you failed an exam, just one; you were out. Even if you came to class without your required homework, you were graciously given your walking papers. During these first four months, there were times when we felt that the sweatshops we'd heard about in the New York Seventh Avenue garment district might be a fair description of our circumstances, except the women at the sewing machines didn't have to empty bedpans.

We rationalized that a certain amount of bellyaching was therapeutic and helped to pull one through a difficult time. Still, we knew we were getting the best possible training and most of us appreciated it. And the cost was reasonable. The twenty-five dollars Daddy borrowed from the bank took care of my uniforms, supplies, food, lodging; everything during the probationary period. Mama sent me a dollar a week and I know it must have been hard on her, but it was a boon to my morale. I was able to go to a little restaurant for a special treat or catch a streetcar and go to the movies. My choice. Once a week.

During the first week, we were given two uniforms each. We all thought they were very smart-looking. The dresses were crisp gray and white striped cotton, with short sleeves and flared skirts, which came to about twelve or thirteen inches from the floor. Over the dresses, we wore a long white cotton pinafore apron, which buttoned in the back. Sturdy, comfortable, low-heel black shoes and black opaque cotton stockings completed the outfit for the first four months.

If you failed the probationary period, you were told that it would be more productive for you to choose another line of work and were sent home. The lucky ones who survived literally the blood, sweat and tears, went through an impressive candlelight capping ceremony. It was a major victory to crow about, because it showed the world that you had crossed the first hurdle of your career. And you looked with envy at the nurses who had already 'made it' and seemed to walk a little taller, sporting their starched, perky, white cotton caps.

After the first few days of orientation, we were required to work floor duty from 7:00 AM to 9:00 AM. This meant assisting the regular nurses with whatever they asked us to do. The most frequently requested assignments were running errands and servicing bedpans. We were not allowed to do anything of any consequence, but just being there and observing gave us a good working knowledge of the everyday operation of the hospital. It provided an introduction to hospital protocol and gave us some idea of what lay ahead.

Morning classes lasted from nine til noon. Twelve to one was lunchtime. Afternoon classes were one to three. Three to four was break time and if you were wise, you used it to study. Four to six was floor duty again. Six to seven was dinner time. Seven to nine was study period. Bedtime was ten o'clock and if you were lucky enough to get in line early for a shower, you had it made. If not, the next morning, you were in trouble, because the six o'clock reveille gave scarcely enough time to bathe and eat breakfast before floor duty at seven. Although you were encouraged to go to bed at ten, the people who set this schedule must have been dreaming. It wasn't unusual for a student to study til the wee hours of the morning and getting the use of the one bathroom was always a challenge.

Despite the hardship, training to become a nurse was a good opportunity for all of the girls in my class. Most of us had nowhere else to turn. A college education was beyond the financial means of our families. College loans were unknown those days. The alternatives were generally to become a clerk in a store, work in a mill or factory of some kind, become a seamstress or a domestic. The low-paying positions as stenographer or secretary did not appeal to any of us and we all felt that we had to pass the required work, and the pressure was intense. Yet, when we were on the floor, we were expected to be bright-eyed and pleasant. I think this period was when I gave some of my finest performances, without the benefit of a stage. It was a maturing experience.

During the first four months, we had only half a day off each week. Time-off was designated on an alternating basis among the students. Weekends were equally strenuous. We worked twelve hours Saturday; ten hours on Sunday, which meant we had two hours off that afternoon.

South Highland was a beautiful hospital in the south side of Birmingham; a three story dark red brick, nestled in a secluded oasis of stately old oak trees. There was a drugstore a few doors away a great place for meeting boys. A block away, there was an Episcopal and a Methodist church. The setting was quiet and serene and if you were unlucky enough to go to a hospital, you could consider yourself fortunate to go to such a pretty, peaceful one; one which had an excellent reputation, and a place I felt proud to be associated with. During the 1930's, Birmingham was a thriving city of over two hundred thousand; large in comparison with my hometown.

South Highland was owned and operated by two brothers, who were doctors: D. S. Moore, Joe Moore and Dr. Prince. They ran a tight, well-organized ship. Its excellent reputation drew the finest specialists in the southeast and physicians from far and wide recommended the hospital to their patients, knowing they would benefit from the medical expertise and latest equipment. Dr. Prince had lost his only son and seemed overwhelmed with grief. Dr. Prince was an excellent surgeon and the fact that his son had died during an operation and he was unable to save him had a devastating effect on him. He was rarely there. Dr. D. S. and Dr. Joe Moore were always on hand and they were good to me, but they were hard taskmasters and I couldn't help thinking they wouldn't have been so demanding, if they had had a daughter.

Neither one did.

The doctors on the staff made an impressive list and they were all excellent teachers. I regret that I can't remember the names of all of them, or even the full names of some of them, but they were were such a fine group of doctors, I'd like to share my memories of a few of them. There was Dr. Joe Hirsch, Internal Medicine, who taught Anatomy. Dr. Garber who taught from his own book on Obstetrics. Dr. Cecil Gaston, Proctology. Dr. Kahn, head of the Orthopedics group, and Dr. Joe Bancroft, Psychiatry. Other areas of medicine represented by specialists included: general surgery, neurosurgery, gynecology, pediatrics, cardiology, radiology, pathology and oncology. All the specialists taught their own particular field. There was also a course on pharmacology taught by a pharmacist. It was called Drugs and Solutions. It provided an introduction to pharmacy and was considered important, because nurses were required to make their own glucose solutions to feed the patients intravenously. There was also a course in dietetics. We learned how to weigh every ounce of food given to diabetic patients and how to create special diets for those with stomach ulcers. South Highland offered a comprehensive course of study for the student nurses, which any nursing facility would be proud of.

I hope I haven't forgotten to give credit where credit is due, and please remember, there are times throughout this book when names are changed to provide privacy.

Chapter 7
THE PROBATION PERIOD

It was rewarding to get to know the outstanding doctors at South Highland and to discover the different facets of their personalities. Some were stiff and formal, even scary. Others were nice and friendly as could be. Dr. Cecil Gaston, proctologist, was one of the later. I liked him very much, despite his quirky sense of humor. Certain allowances should be made for anybody who has to look up the posterior entries of the alimentary canal all day.

Dr. Gaston had a little practical joke he liked to play on the new student nurses in his first class.

Two eager, naïve girls were always the hapless victims of this unique sense of humor and I was unfortunate to be one of them.

After the basic introduction, Dr. Gaston announced, "I want," he hesitated in order to look at the names of the new trainees then continued, "Miss Perkins and Miss Robbins to sit on the front row to help with an important demonstration."

We followed his instructions with nervous apprehension. We knew he would be talking mainly about doing proctoscopies and hemmoridectomies, the procedures, which dealt with probing the anal canal to check for growths or other abnormalities and the removal of hemorrhoids. The idea of serving for a demonstration about either of these procedures produced instant panic.

Dr. Gaston enjoyed himself thoroughly as he explained how he wanted his patients cared for before and after surgery. To aid in his lecture, he had a funny-looking portable sit-in lavatory, or johnny bowl. He explained, "Ladies, this is a sitz bath bowl. Sitz bath comes form the German word 'sitz,' which means the act of sitting; plus 'bad,' (pronounced BAHD) which means bath. In other words, you sit to bathe the bottom only, whereas in a regular bath tub, there is plenty of room to bathe

55

the entire body." I had a flashback to the cramped quarters of the portable tubs we used at home and silently questioned the accuracy of his statement that bathtubs have plenty of room. Not all of them did.

He continued, "The sitz solution is to be placed in the bowl, followed by the patient. The patient is to be very gently rolled around in the warm solution, which is soothing to a sore derriere. This is frequently done several times a day and you must be careful about how you handle the patient, so you don't slosh the solution all over everything."

In addition to his other talents, Dr. Gaston had created his own ointments for his patients. There was Gaston Number One and Gaston Number Two. These he discussed at length. "After the sitz bath, you are to gently apply the prescribed Gaston Number One or Two to the wounded area. You must be sure that you use the correct ointment and you must discard any feelings of embarrassment in the application process. Just remember the patient is in pain and will welcome this soothing procedure. To alleviate any further distress about handling the sitz bath, please remember this treatment will be done by the male orderlies for the male patients." There was an audible sigh of relief upon receiving this information.

Dr. Gaston rambled on and on as the clock on the wall approached the end of class. I felt like it was also hastening the time of my doom, because he had not yet called for the demonstration mentioned at the beginning of his lecture. I sneaked a side-glance at my co-demonstrator. She looked ashen.

Dr. Gaston had a definite gleam in his eye as he looked at the clock. Having just met the man, I didn't know what that gleam meant and it increased my feeling of insecurity. He continued, "Now, let us talk for a few minutes about enemas," and my heart sank. "The procedure of administering an enema is of utmost importance to my patients, who are being prepared for surgery. The word enema is derived from a Greek word, which means to inject, to send in. In this case, we inject a liquid into the intestine to urge it to empty and cleanse the lower gastrointestinal tract. This is done, not only for hygienic purposes, but also to delay intestinal peristaltic action. Peristalsis is the involuntary movement within the intestinal tract, which forces waste matter out of the body. The enema is not always pleasant because it can sometimes precipitate cramping, but after it's all over the patient feels better. Now, in order to show you how I want my enemas to be given, I'm going to demonstrate on one of the girls here."

I felt almost faint, when I heard the bell signaling the end of class. Mama had never spanked the imagination out of me and I could just hear him say, "Miss Perkins, if you will, please turn around this way," while he put my head and feet together and directed my bottom toward the class. Instead, he smiled.

"Ladies, unfortunately, the demonstration will have to wait." His timing was perfect. And I could have killed him.

Of course, the demonstration never took place. Later, I learned that this practical joke was a standard procedure with Dr. Gaston and his new trainees. At first, I was mad, but after a while, I forgave him and learned to appreciate him for his gentle nature and medical expertise, despite an occasional lapse with his weird humor.

Another teacher, who won the heart of many of the nurses was Dr. Garber, whose specialty was obstetrics and gynecology. They were of keen interest to a bunch of naïve young women, because they dealt not only with sex, buy also with the result of this activity. Although there was no sex education in the schools, most of us had found out from one source or another that babies could result from sexual intercourse. I remember there was one girl, who wasn't quite sure how it all took place. She was soon informed.

In this class, we found out that gynecology deals primarily with non-pregnant women, their diseases and the importance of hygiene. Dr. Garber elevated the birds and bees theory to a lofty plane with his eloquent lectures. He was forthright in his information about the dangers of syphilis and gonorrhea. We didn't have the help of penicillin or any of the other powerful antibiotics available today, and sexually transmitted diseases weren't anything to be taken lightly. He was also inspiring in his belief that human sexuality could and should be considered a wondrous gift from God and practiced accordingly. He handled the delicate subject with such finesse and in such an articulate manner, before we knew it, we were well-informed students, with a minimum of blushes.

Dr. Garber could have been on the stage. He interspersed his lectures with occasional time-worn jokes and corny platitudes. He freely offered bits of religious wisdom and comments on ethics, virtue, aesthetics, morality and judgement. He was the author of numerous poems, inspired by nineteenth century romanticism and sentimentality. I never saw a teacher enjoy himself more than he did. Having a captive audience in the student nurses, he took full advantage of the opportunity and happily shared his creativity. Sometimes, he closed the class with one of his heartthrobs; his emotional delivery intensifying as the tears and hankies appeared.

The nurses loved it; he loved it, and everybody was happy. There was one poem I vaguely remember; a poem which left not a dry eye in the room. It was titled "Everlasting Love" and told the story of a young pregnant woman whose husband was fighting in France during World War One and as she was praying for him to return to her and their unborn child, he was killed. Dr. Garber's intention was to make the statement that love outlasts death and is eternal. The cynics in the class interpreted it as meaning that sometimes God says "No," and we were already beginning to see that in the infirmary. Nevertheless, it was a real tear-jerker.

Dr. Garber was not the best poet, but he was sensitive, bright and fun to listen to as he taught us about the growth of babies in the womb. And you could tell that he had great compassion, when he talked about the complications which could arise during pregnancy, such as extra-uterine conception, when the fetus forms outside the womb, uremic poisoning, the occasional birth of monsters, and abortions.

There were no abortion clinics in those days and whatever your moral, ethical, or religious views, if a woman unfortunately conceived out of wedlock, she had several options and none of them were good. She could go quietly out of town and have the baby in an area where she was unknown, put the infant up for adoption, or return home with a baby, who was claimed to be the child of the girl's mother, aunt, or some other generous female. She could go out of town and have an abortion performed by either an experienced doctor who charged an exorbitant amount, or to a quack, distant or local, with frequently life threatening results. Or she could stay at home, have the child with both of them suffering the humiliating condemnation of the community.

Dr. Garber's words made a strong impression on the students. He used to say, "It's a strange thing about abortions and the tenacity of life within the womb. There have been women, who have wanted to bring on an abortion and have tried all types of physical activity, such as hard riding on horseback, jumping up and down; jumping from dangerously high places, and nothing happens. That little baby girl or boy sticks in there as fast as glue. In other cases, there are women who want desperately to have a little one, and one day, for no apparent reason they will start bleeding and loose the child."

As I said, Dr. Garber had written his own textbook. Naturally, we used it.

Chapter 8
CAPPED BY CANDLELIGHT

The probationary period kept us constantly on the go with never a dull moment. Life went so fast with all the demands made on our time, the days seemed to run one into another and I can't remember everything, but there are several scenes which remain vivid. One made an impression, because I thought surely I'd be expelled.

The accident occurred during one of the rare times when I wasn't in my nurse's uniform and it caused considerable stir. I was wearing my one woolen suit, flirting with some boy in the parlor when I spilled my drink down the front of me. I was distressed, but I felt that I could cope with the situation with one of Mama's fine home remedies.

Having come from a small town where there was no dry cleaning establishment, Mama had taught me how to clean my woolen clothes with gasoline and hang them outside to dry. Naturally, I had brought a bottle of gasoline along with me to the hospital. Thoughtlessly, I cleaned my nice suit with the gasoline without taking into consideration that there was no designated place outside to put it. A nail on the wall in back of my cot, took care of a hanging place and the room was so large and airy, I felt sure the matter was well in hand. I was wrong.

The quick reaction from my roommates was disturbing.

"Good grief! What's going on here?" "It smells awful in here!" "Phew!" These were the more gentle comments.

I turned the other way and tried to pretend this wasn't happening, but the odor was like a magnet drawing attention to the source of the fragrance.

"Birdie! Get that smelly thing out of here!." The complaints continued and I shouted, "There's no place else to put it!." I withstood their slings and arrows and there it hung, perfuming the dorm room with its pungent odor, which spread through the open door down the hall to lend its distinctive fragrance to all passing by.

It was embarrassing; and the embarrassment grew as Jake, the fat little hospital engineer happened to be one of those passing by and got a whiff. He dashed down the hall, gave a rapid knock by the side of the door and huffed and puffed his way into the room.

He shouted, "Somebody's about to start a fire down here!"

His eyes darted in every direction and his head bobbed around as he sniffed the air.

"Where's the gasoline?"

It was an unnecessary question, for in the next second, his nose led him straight to my cot. I stood there petrified as he snatched my smelly suit and small bottle of gasoline and quickly carried them both outside the back entrance. As he made his hasty retreat, he shook a wild finger at me and yelled.

"Don't you ever do this a gin!"

I was terrified for fear he would report me and I would be expelled, but he turned out to have a compassionate heart in that little round body. He never said another word about it to me, Miss Smith or anybody. We did have a brief lecture on fire safety not long afterwards, but that was the end of it. It was also the end of my indoor dry cleaning operation.

A lot of things helped ease the daily grind during the probationary period. I have always liked people and enjoyed getting to know the other students, the registered nurses, the practical nurses we worked with on floor duty; the doctors and all the staff. The hospital personnel represented a wide cross section of society and despite the differences in personality and background, we gradually acquired the feeling of a caring community, working together and, in most cases, tried to help each other. Naturally, there were some conflicting personalities, often obvious feelings of hierarchy and there was one particularly strong character who ruled the roost in the kitchen. You'll meet this charmer a little later.

Somehow, the first four months passed by. They ended in joy and relief for those of us who passed and in pain and embarrassement for the two who failed.

The candlelight capping ceremony was a very special occasion. The service was held in a church a block away from South Highland. Families were invited to attend and I was thrilled to have Mama and Lema come all the one hundred and ten miles from Vernon to witness my 'capping'. A dear little great aunt, Aunt Hattie, who lived in Birmingham, was also kind enough to come.

It was a happy time and everything was beautiful. The ten candidates were immaculate in freshly starched uniforms. Eager smiling faces glowed in the soft candlelight from two large standing candelabra, which flanked either side of the presentation table. A formal wedding had taken place the night before and the lovely floral decorations were left for us to enjoy. There was even an organist, who played some of the old-time favorite hymns to put everybody in an inspired mood.

The preacher of the church welcomed us and gave the invocation. Miss Oster, who guided us through our course of study, was the first speaker. She was particularly proud because we were her first class at South Highland. The beautiful Miss Augusta Ann Smith spoke briefly and said nice things about our courage and determination and introduced Dr. D. S. Moore, who gave the main address. After his message of praise and encouragement to face the future with a determined heart and mind, he asked us to come forward as our names were called. I was so excited, I don't remember anything except him saying "Miss Birdie Perkins." Miss Smith placed my new nurse's cap on my head and if it had been a golden crown, I don't think I could have been happier.

With my mop of red hair, there was no problem anchoring the crisp, white cotton cap and everybody else managed to balance their new headgear satisfactorily, with the exception of one girl, who didn't have enough hair to hold it and it kept sliding askew. But, by then, we were all so pleased with ourselves; we were in a kindly mood and tried not to notice.

After the capping ceremony, we were paid $7.50 a month for riotous living for the next thirty-two months of training. This was the first salary I received from my chosen career and I felt like I was really on my way. In my heart, I knew how Hannibal felt when he crossed his first mountain.

My living quarters were elevated from the basement dorm to a large wooden building across from the emergency room. The building housed sixty nurses through their three year course of study. A welcome addition to my daily life was the presence of a dear, kindly housemother, Mrs. Sloan and I now had a nice room, which I shared with two other student nurses. It was far from glamorous, but it had the basics: three single beds, three dressers and three closets. There were also three bath-commode accommodations; however, these were down the hall, shared by all the nurses on the floor. There were twenty-five to thirty nurses on the floor, so you can imagine the fun. Plumbing facilities were on the scant side at South Highland.

One of my roommates was Emma Frances Inzer, a beautiful, tall, slender blond from Eden, Alabama. She had delicate lovely features, tiny hands and a smile that made you feel everything was going to be all right. She had such a gentle manner, it was obvious she was born to brighten lives of others. We both came from small towns. We had a lot in common. In the old dorm room, Emma's bed had been on one side of me, with Ruth Deramus close by.

Ruth and Emma were my roommates in our new quarters and they were as different as night and day. By the furthest stretch of the imagination, you could not call Ruth sexy or glamorous. She was a medium height, stocky girl, with hazel eyes and brown hair flying in all directions. Ruth had her own distinctive personality, which sometimes threw people off track about the really large heart she housed. She was simply a young woman of intense feelings and was never shy about expressing her views. She was one of the most opinionated persons I have ever known and could flare up at a moment's notice. These minor explosions were guaranteed to occur, when we got an O.B. (obstetrics) call in the middle of the night summoning us to action for the arrival of a new citizen of Alabama. Immediately, Ruth wound up and started spouting her theory about the reproductive process.

She fumed: "The reason we have to get up to greet these new arrivals at such an ungodly hour is because that's when their parents got them started. They should start the reproductive process at a decent hour instead of two or three o'clock in the morning!" She was a woman of strong convictions.

I shall never forget our first encounter the day we both arrived at South Highland.

She came in even later than I. All the new trainees were in our dormitory room getting ready for bed, when the door opened and Mrs. Smith smilingly said, "Girls, this is your new roommate, Ruth Deramus." and quickly departed. Ruth came blustering in, burdened down with baggage of various sizes, bumping into everything in her path, mad as a hornet, displaying a remarkable vocabulary.

"What a hellova way to get started! Of all the crap to have to put up with. You'd think that old buzzard Henry Ford would put a better grade of tires on a truck. Here I've been riding since daybreak and how many damned flat tires do you think we had?" The question was directed at no one in particular, so no one answered and she went on fuming and fussing, while we all watched in fascinated disbelief at this strange new addition to our midst.

"Not one damned tire. Not two damned tires. Not three infernal tires!" She paused and looked around with flashing eyes to see what kind of response she was getting from her audience. "Four damned tires went flat! Left me smelling like a billy goat and starving, with no dinner!" She threw her bundle of bags all over the bed and turned a scowling countenance toward me, as I extended an apple and banana I'd brought from home. I smiled and said, "Hi, I'm Birdie Perkins."

Well, the clouds disappeared like magic, as she displayed an enormous grin, gave a salute with a big ham of a hand, which had valiantly changed four tires in the course of a day, and I knew we were going to be friends.

Chapter 9
BREAKING POINT

Quotas are common in the business world, particularly among those who work in sales. You don't think of them being imposed in the nursing field, but they were in the long-ago 1930's and I expect they still are, especially during the training period. The quotas we had were for 'scrubs.' A 'scrub' was the cleaning procedure you went through prior to assisting with an operation.

About fifteen minutes before a nurse was due to be in the operating room, she went into a small 'scrub room'; put on a sterile mask and cap to cover her hair completely and used a little brush to scrub her hands and nails to get them as clean as possible. This was not a quickie one-minute procedure. You were expected to scrub and scrub some more; not just the hands, but all the way up your arms. When your fingers started getting wrinkles in them and you felt you had eliminated as many unseen creatures and germs as possible, you were ready for an assistant to put on your green cotton sterile gown and sterile rubber gloves.

As I recall, I had to do approximately a hundred and eighty scrubs one summer. This was a major responsibility in my weekly schedule and the steam bath I got in the over-heated operating room made me feel exhausted most of the time. The temperature could go over a steaming one hundred degrees in the operating room in the summer. It was a killer. An apendectomy might last only a couple of hours, but major brain surgery could start at seven A.M. and continue all day. During these long sessions the operating team would be literally dripping sweat and an assistant stood close by to give a salt tablet and a sip of coke to alleviate the weakness that could hit you and make you feel faint.

In addition to all this stress, at the end of the surgery, the nurses had to prepare for the next day's operations. The hospital had huge metal tanks called autoclaves. We had to place all the instruments, equipment and bandages to be used in surgery the next day in one of these big steam sterilizers and at the end of a long day, it was a final duty hard to cope with. Only a young woman in good physical, mental and emotional condition could stand the constant strain.

I still feel sad when I think of what happened to one young nurse who didn't have the stamina to continue the demanding schedule. This girl knew that she might be dismissed and the heartache and disgrace was more than she could stand. Evidently, she also had some other problems, so she handled the situation the only way she knew how.

Sally Jo (not her real name) was a lively, attractive brunette. She was the one who always had a smile and an optimistic outlook, even on the blackest days. She was the one you could always turn to for an unfailing word of encouragement when something had you down. She'd always smile and put her arm around you and say the right thing like, "It's going to be better. Just wait and see." She was so darn nice and pleasant all the time; everybody loved Sally Jo and looked up to her as a role model and an inspiration.

During the second summer of training, Sally Jo was acting more exhilarated than usual and it seemed to several of us that there was a shade of falseness in her enthusiasm. We knew she'd been hanging around a married doctor more than the necessary daily contact called for and we worried about her. We also knew that her grades had fallen and if they fell much more, Sally Jo would be heading back to her small hometown, without her diploma as a registered nurse. We worried, but we hoped it was just a passing phase and that she'd come to her senses about the futility of fooling around with a man who belonged to somebody else. We kidded her a little, but she passed it off lightly and kept up a false front without batting an eye.

The last Sunday afternoon in August is indelibly impressed in my memory.

The night before, Sally Jo and I had night duty in the nursery, working from seven P.M. Saturday until seven A.M. Sunday. I still remember how lovely Sally Jo was that night. She seemed to have a certain glow about her as she cared for the tiny infants, soothing the restless ones with tender words, picking up and rocking in her arms the distressed little creatures who were not adjusted to the big world they'd so recently entered, and I remember how gently she changed their diapers and lovingly and tenderly carried them to their mothers to nurse. We left the nursery a few minutes after seven and were leaving the infirmary, when the doctor Sally Jo liked spoke to her and I left them talking together in the hall.

When we had this schedule, we'd sleep til around four in the afternoon. This gave us time to wash our hair and relax awhile before eating and reporting to work at seven P.M.

My roommates and I had just finished dressing, when Sally Jo came waltzing into our room and suggested enthusiastically, "Let's go to the parlor and have a Coke!" It sounded like a good idea, so Emma Frances, Ruth, and a couple of other nurses on the floor and I went to the front room of the dormitory to share experiences and opinions about nursing and boyfriends, which were our two main topics of conversation.

Sally Jo looked especially pretty that afternoon, almost like a wax doll, and unusually vivacious as she raised her Coke bottle and made a toast. "Here's to all of you! Here's to South Highland and its wonderful doctors!" With a flourish, she drank the contents of the bottle and as we sat there dumbfounded, she collapsed.

Her "coke" was one hundred percent Lysol!

Within minutes she was behind closed doors in the emergency room. None of us were allowed to enter, but knowing what we did about what this powerful disinfectant could do to your insides, it must have been awful. Although she had immediate attention she never regained consciousness. She lived about thirty minutes.

There were whispers and a lot of conjecture, but we never knew for sure why Sally Jo chose to end her life when it was just beginning. Her parents forbade an autopsy. Her suicide was distressing to all the hospital staff, particularly the nurses. We thought if only we had known her real state of mind, maybe we could have done something to help her. She had always done so much to help us with her kind ways and encouragement and we all felt a certain guilt.

Those of us who were closely associated with Sally Jo were demoralized by her death and for a while, there was more than usual talk about suicide and we talked about another case which had happened earlier. A lovely private nurse took some unknown potion to get relief from the stress she was going through and they found her dead in her bed. Several times she had said, "If I ever decide to end my life, no one will ever be able to tell how I did it." It was a true statement. An autopsy was performed, but medicine was not as advanced as it is now and the exact cause of death was never determined.

I also remembered another nurse who overdosed on a medication. She went into a coma for a few days, but she was lucky. She survived her attempted suicide and when she regained consciousness she was sent to a sanitarium in Mississippi. She never returned to South Highland.

The nurses who saw a fellow worker take her life or attempt to end it all were genuinely distressed. No matter how hard you tried to accept it, each case was demoralizing and frightening. Still the death of Sally Jo was particularly hard to accept.

We never knew for sure why she took her life, nor why she chose such a horribly painful way to leave us.

She was so lovely.

Chapter 10

SWEATING IT OUT IN SURGERY

The summer that Sally Jo left us was surely the most severe during the entire three year-training program. I'm five feet six and during this period, my weight dropped down to ninety pounds. I was skin and bones and showed the effects of the long hours we were required to work. And the discipline was harsh. If we made a mistake, we had to work twelve hours instead of ten. At the same time, we still had to have our homework done for the next day's class or face the prospect of being expelled. It was a grueling schedule made more difficult because there was no air conditioning.

In our pampered society, it is hard to get the real feeling of working in extreme heat day after day and how debilitating it is. Only those who have had a taste of this experience can nod their heads and say, "I know. I've been there." True, there are a few hardy souls who have no use for air conditioning and there are reports about the hazards of germs being spread through the vents, but I expect most folks would opt for the cool comfort.

South Highland's operating room was well-equipped for the period, but it had the unfortunately accurate reputation of being the hottest place outside hell. The heat was so intense, it seemed to penetrate to the very center of your bones. The rotating fans tried valiantly, but all they did was circulate the hot air. Out of curiosity, a nurse hid a thermometer on the floor, propped up against the leg of a table against the wall. Most of the nurses knew where it was. I was one of them and can vouch for it going up to a hundred and four a number of times in late August and early September. That's what it was on the floor, but heat rises and we weren't lying around on the cooler level.

Assisting in surgery on such days was grueling. The surgeons, being human, also found it difficult, especially for the lengthy procedures. And the stress was worse if the doctor was in a foul frame of mind to begin with. South Highland had high standards for its doctors, but as in every other line of work, mistakes happen; doctors can use poor judgement just like mere mortals. Or a good man may reach a breaking point. I remember one very hot day in September I was scheduled for a 'scrub' for a delicate brain operation, which would probably take ten hours.

One of the nurses wheeled in the patient on a portable table; a lovely woman in her fifties. A brain tumor was causing her to lose her eyesight and had the potential of being fatal. She had already been given a sedative and had a nice buzz on when the anesthesiologist administered the drug which would keep her unconscious during the surgery. Quite a few people were taking part in this operation. The star of the show, of course, was the surgeon, who has since gone to his reward and shall remain nameless. He was assisted by a couple of interns. The anesthesiologist had to monitor the patient during the entire operation. Then there were several assisting nurses. I was one of them.

Those taking part in the surgery all wore a head covering, mask and gloves. This extra clothing made it all the worse when it was hot and I began to sweat. Everybody began to sweat and the operating room supervisor was kept busy mopping brows and giving out salt tablets and cokes to keep us from passing out. Everything went along fine during the morning hours, but as the afternoon temperature rose in the operating room, so did the surgeon's temper. He started to encounter unexpected complications and the scene began to get lively. The surgeon lost his cool and put on a performance such as I have never seen before or since. He began with a small flow of cuss words scarcely audible under his mask. Those of us who had worked with him before knew him to be a volatile man and we prayed that things would not go from bad to worse.

They did. The small stream gradually erupted into a raging flood of unrestrained profanity. Instead of handing the instruments to me when he had finished with them, he started tossing them flamboyantly in the air. I started jumping and ducking, attempting to dodge his discarded instruments while trying to hand the next ones as he called for them. And I was not alone in these bodily movements; his entire team looked like they were quietly doing some strange, esoteric dance around him. Only the patient was immobile and fortunately, she was unable to witness the ritual. Finally, he started sewing up the incision and said curtly, "Cut here." I cut where he instructed and instantly he jumped up and down in a rage with his fists in the air, tore off his mask showing his contorted features. He glared at me and screamed, "You cut the sutures too God damn short!" and stormed out of the room. I thought surely I would faint.

It's hard enough when you have things going smoothly, with a surgeon in command of himself and the situation. When you've gone for nearly ten hours with no lunch break in the debilitating, oppressive heat of South Highland's 'sweat box' and have the surgeon go beserk, toss instruments and scream at you, it's unnerving. It's hazardous to both the patient and the operating team.

I am happy to relate the patient survived and later got back her vision. Those of us who assisted in the operation also survived.

To my knowledge, the hospitals nowadays don't allow such histrionics. Back then, it was not unusual for a surgeon to play the prima donna and throw a fit when he got frustrated and none of the underlings dared cross him. Things had to get pretty bad for somebody to report a doctor's indiscretion.

Concerning the flamboyant surgeon in the episode just described; I wasn't the one who squealed, but somebody must have, because shortly thereafter, I heard through the hospital grapevine that he was encouraged to take a one-year sabbatical for rest, recreation and further study in neurosurgery and self control. I never saw him again, but I wish him well. He was basically a good surgeon. If he hadn't been, that lady would never have regained her eyesight.

Chapter 11

PUTTING IT IN & TAKING IT OUT

Since we're all human, we all make mistakes. I think I was a little slow in accepting this possible failing in my own character, although I was quite observant about its occurrence in others and prided myself on my compassion. Then one day I pulled a royal boner, which couldn't be hidden under the table or anywhere else. It was a blatant, careless miscalculation, which was in no way life-threatening, but it was a boo-boo of such magnitude, it affected all of the hospital staff and a number of the patients. I'm sure the entire staff remembered it for at least a week and probably made less than understanding remarks out of earshot, because the ones which drifted my way were not ego-building. I think only Dr. Moore stood by me. The error in judgement was decidedly my fault and when it happened, I could only hope for the memory to soon fade. After all, nobody's perfect.

It began one day when Miss Augusta Ann Smith sent word for me to report to her office. She smiled. I think Miss Smith was always smiling. She said, "Miss Perkins, we have run into a minor difficulty and I'm sure I can count on you to help us. Please sit down."

I sat and it's a good thing I did, because I was stunned by her request, which I knew good and well, despite all the smiling, was an order. She continued, "Mrs. Shaffer, the dietician, (I think that was her name) is going out of town for a two month course of study and in discussing this matter with Dr. Moore, we have decided that you are capable of assuming her responsibilities while she's away." Miss Smith was still smiling when she finished. She had her usual appearance of serenity, just like this was the most logical solution you could imagine.

It hit me like a ton of bricks. I protested, "Miss Smith, I don't think I can handle that." It did no good.

Miss Smith tried to be gentle in the way she handled the matter, but I could tell by the way she was talking, her mind was made up and there was no way to escape. "You made excellent grades in your dietetic courses. You'll simply put into practice all the things you have learned. We'll give you extra council and a lot of moral support. Just remember, you can call on me for advice anytime you need me."

That ended the conversation. It did not; however, end my serious need for close guidance and at the crucial time when I needed Miss Smith, she was not there. I know she didn't mean to desert me after throwing me out into the cold hard world of dietetics and meal preparation for nearly a hundred people, but that's the way it happened.

For the next two months, I was in charge of all the special diets; that is, the meals for the diabetic and ulcer patients and anyone else on a restricted diet. I was also in charge of planning and ordering food for the entire hospital staff.

Mr. Branch, the kind person, who never reported my using gasoline to clean a suit and a man I considered to be my friend, bought the groceries each day for the hospital. He went to the farmers' market first thing in the morning to select fruit and vegetables while they were at their peak of freshness. Every morning, his first words to me were, "Miss Perkins, what do you want me to buy today?" The day of the disaster, I gave him a list and added at the last minute, "I also want twelve dozen bunches of turnip greens."

Mr. Branch looked at me. "Miss Perkins, are you sure you want twelve dozen bunches of turnip greens?"

I said, "Yes. Twelve dozen bunches of turnip greens. That should do it." It did and then some.

About an hour and a half later, a sturdy, stoic, black woman, who had worked in the hospital kitchen many years, came to me. She said, "Miss Perkins, will you please come downstairs. I want to show you somethin'." She had a concerned look.

"What is it you want to show me, Sarah?"

"Miss Perkins, I don't much think I can describe it. It's somethin' you gonna have to see for yo'self."

We went together down to the Ice Cream Room, a small room, a very small room, which was originally used for making and storing ice cream. It was now used to store fresh fruits and vegetables since it was one of the coolest places in the building; but it was still called the Ice Cream

Room. I took one look at the display before me and felt the blood rush to my face.

Turnip greens were everywhere! One hundred and forty-four bunches to be exact! They covered every available counter and table space. They were on the tables, under the tables, stacked almost up to the ceiling in some places and stacked against the wall in others. I had never seen so many turnip greens in all my life and I wailed, "Oh, my Lord, what'll I do?"

Mr. Branch poked his head around the door and observed his purchase with pride. "I bought out the whole market!" Sarah gave me a couple of sympathetic pats on the shoulder and said, "I expect you'll wanna go have a talk with somebody soon as you can. They say confession is good for the soul. It's also good for findin' out what to do with twelve dozen bunches of turnip greens!"

I dashed out to find Miss Smith, but Miss Smith was nowhere to be found! She was not there during my hour of need, which meant I had to face Dr. Moore with my blunder.

I ran to his office and his secretary announced me. As a rule, I didn't sit in the presence of a doctor without an invitation, much less the chief administrator of the hospital, but my knees had turned to butter and I sat in the first available chair.

I'm sure he suspected something had gone wrong, before I said a word. We had had a couple of talks before when things had not gone as anticipated.

The words rushed out. "Dr. Moore, I have done something awful! It was a mistake. I didn't mean to do it and I don't know how it happened, but I'm sorry and I promise it won't happen again, and I need your advice."

He lowered his glasses on his nose and looked over them at me, "What is it you're not going to do again, Miss Perkins?"

"I am not going to order twelve dozen bunches of turnip greens again!" I paused a moment to see if he was going to yell at me, but he just sat there and looked at me. Dr. Moore always had the instincts of a gentleman.

"Dr. Moore, they're all over the Ice Cream Room! They're all over everywhere! They're almost up to the ceiling. There are enough turnip greens to feed an army. And I can't take them back!"

Dr. Moore perked up and without a pause, he said brightly, "That's all right, Miss Perkins. A certain amount of turnip greens are healthy for you. They provide iron and a lot of trace elements. Tell the cook to serve turnip greens to the staff every day for the next week and I'll see to it that they eat them. They'll also do for some of the patients. There are a few I can think of; it might improve their disposition." After this meeting, I always had a soft spot in my heart for Dr. D. S. Moore.

Nobody asked me, but I felt this work in dietetics was a big responsibility to put on a twenty-one year old nurse, but I did the best I knew how. In a couple of days, I knew Miss Smith had heard about my boo-boo; she could scarcely have avoided it. She was the soul of diplomacy, which means she didn't mention it. And I continued to grow in dietetic wisdom. I learned to cope with other minor emergencies, like the Sunday morning when I went to the kitchen to check on the food and discovered that the meat for the mid-day meal was missing. There are just so many places you can look for meat at South Highland and most of them are in the huge refrigerators.

This called for immediate action.

The meat market was responsible for this error and even though it was Sunday, I wasn't going to allow the patients and staff to forfeit their entree. I knew the owner was probably at church a block away, so I sent one of the kitchen workers to roust him from the nap he reportedly took during the sermon. When the usher whispered to the owner that someone from the hospital wanted a word with him, he jumped up and dashed to his market. He must have done some mighty fast scurrying, because in less than an hour, he personally delivered the lost meat. The folks at South Highland never knew how close they came to having vegetable soup for dinner that Sunday. The distressed owner felt very bad about the mishap. The hospital gave him a lot of business and he didn't want to lose it.

I prided myself on how nice I was to him about his error. It gives you a good feeling to observe human frailty in others, especially, when you've matured enough to admit you've made a few blunders of your own along the way.

Working at South Highland provided a good education in the art of interpersonal relationships. Some people like Miss Smith could weather the worst kinds of emotional storms without getting perturbed. On the other hand, there was Edna.

Edna was the head cook; a tall, large black woman, with big brown eyes shining out of a round determined face that brooked no nonsense from man nor beast. She pulled her black hair up tight in a knot on top of her head. She wore a white cotton cap, required by the hospital, and when she left the kitchen and removed the cap, the knot made an interesting hairdo, but with the cap on, the concealed knot looked like a strange growth. One day, a new employee, who had not been informed about Edna's volatile temper, made light of her topknot. It seems the light-hearted young black man made a disparaging remark about Edna's mental agility and asked her when the egg she was incubating on top of her head was going to hatch.

Edna did not take that remark in good humor. She had at her disposal a long, lethal-looking butcher knife and when the young man lit into Edna with his teasing, Edna lit into him flashing that butcher knife around in a manner to put fear in the bravest. She chased him all the way out the hospital and that was the last we ever saw of him.

Protocol, rules and regulations, and obedience to your superiors were strongly emphasized at South Highland and I didn't mind following orders from above. I didn't have any gripe with the threat of dismissal, while in training or afterwards. I didn't mind following all the rules and regulations. I didn't mind jumping like a jack-in-the-box, whenever I was seated and a doctor approached, but I know I would never have put up with anyone threatening me with a butcher knife. I also know that I wouldn't tease my superiors and question their mental acumen or their good taste in hairstyle.

Even if you ran across an occasional lemon, most of the staff at South Highland were competent and agreeable and there were a few doctors and nurses, with a strong sense of duty, compassion and generosity, who were an outstanding credit to their profession. One surgeon who easily comes in this category was Dr. Clayton Stiles.

He had soft grey eyes and a winning smile which instilled a sense of confidence in his ability. You just knew when you got to see Dr. Stiles, he'd help you. His area of expertise was removing foreign objects from the esophagus, stomach, and lungs. It's amazing how many people swallow or inhale things they're not supposed to. Babies, small children and the elderly weren't the only ones; there were plenty of people in the prime of life who had these accidents.

The most prevalent offenders of the stomach were straight pins, open safety pins, small pieces of glass, and needles. (We had one lady come in and request that a fly she swallowed be removed. An emetic took good care of this.) Some of the serious intrusions into the lungs were small bones, peanuts, grains of corn, and, in the summer, watermelon seed. If the air passages were blocked, you could suffocate in a matter of minutes and be on your way to your reward. If the object settled in your lungs, Dr. Stiles was the best surgeon you could possibly want. His fame had spread and doctors all over the southeast sent their patients to him when time allowed, and you could consider yourself lucky if you were close by.

Dr. Stiles had developed his technique to an enviable state of the art. One of the instruments he designed was a thin, metal stick, which he had made in several lengths, from twelve to eighteen inches long. He inserted this in the area where the alien object lay in wait. The instrument had a funny-looking spoon-shaped end, which reminded me of a duck's bill. The doctor inserted it to the foreign object, scooped it up and pulled it out. He performed this difficult procedure with remarkable finesse.

When I assisted Dr. Stiles with one of these delicate operations, I had to kneel down and get in a position like I was praying. He would tilt the head of the operating table down to get a good view of where he was going, while I knelt beside him and held a bright light to help him see the way. He also had the benefit of extra wattage from a light attached to a leather headband. I really don't know how he was able to remove those objects. For many procedures, today's surgeons have x-ray equipment that lets them watch which way they're going. Back then, a doctor could look at an x-ray, but after that he was on his own. I always thought Dr. Stiles had a God-given gift that made him so skillful. The procedure was difficult and awkward to perform, but Dr. Stiles saved many lives. I have great respect and admiration for this doctor.

Most of his patients were able to leave the infirmary the same day or the next, like my little cousin, who was rushed into the emergency room after inhaling a safety pin while sewing. Others had to stay longer and he was very conscientious about looking after them. And if a patient couldn't afford a private nurse and he thought the patient needed one, I've seen him hire a nurse at his own expense.

He was a dedicated man and his patients loved him.

Chapter 12

AN UNFORGETTABLE GRADUATION GIFT

Evidently, my superiors were pleased with my performance as a student nurse, because a month before graduation, I was promoted to Floor Supervisor and with this rise in status I was given a room, a salary of sixty dollars a month and the privilege of doing private duty.

Graduation came and went joyfully three years after I entered the training program at South Highland Infirmary. It was a memorable occasion with friends and relatives on hand to acknowledge our accomplishment and pass along well-deserved congratulations. There were some twenty girls who received their diplomas; fresh-faced and eager to enter the needed ranks of registered nurses. We may have been a little afraid of the future, but basically, we knew we had been well trained and looked forward to our mission of mercy. We had struggled through a tiresome, two-day Alabama state examination, which licensed us in Alabama, with a reciprocal arrangement for licensing in other states, if we wanted to relocate.

Although Birmingham was a small town, it had an airport and occasionally, some of us would go there on a pretty Sunday afternoon and watch the activity. There was an older man, a pilot somewhere in his thirties, who took a shine to the nurses and was always showing off for us with loop-t-loops and flying upside down and a lot of other dare-devil maneuvers. He was a nice guy, the son of a doctor in Birmingham, but he just couldn't help trying to get attention. Well, a few days after graduation, he came to the hospital and said he wanted to give the girls in my class an airplane ride as a graduation gift. We were so excited, we just about exploded and if we'd known what was going to happen, we probably would have.

The following Sunday at the appointed time, he showed up and with hospital approval, he drove ten of us in an ambulance to the airport. You never heard such happy chattering and laughter from a bunch of young women thrilled from head-tip to toe-tips over the prospect of their first ride in an airplane. And the happy pilot was chattering and laughing just about as much as the girls.

At the airport, he lined us up and said he'd take us one after another for a ten-minute ride. My classmate at that time, Montez Downs, was the first in line and we watched in fascination as the pilot put goggles on her and strapped her into the little two-seater with an open cockpit. They took off and soon became a little dot in the sky and we waited and looked at other folks coming and going. When our pilot returned, Montez wasn't with him. He said he had let her out at the terminal.

I was the second one to go up and I was so excited I could scarcely stand it. All my life I had wanted to fly in a plane and the fact that my dream was becoming a reality was pushing my adrenaline to maximum production. The happy, friendly pilot put the goggles on me, strapped me in and off we went into the wild blue yonder. For the first few minutes, I was giggling and laughing and shouting, trying to get acclimated while we went higher and higher.

Suddenly, I found myself upside down looking at the earth below. My goggles didn't allow me to see clearly and it was a weird feeling, like I was suspended in space. Without warning, he started doing loop-t-loops one after another, whereupon I lost my sense of equilibrium. I lost my laughter. I lost my good disposition. I lost my delicious chicken and dumpling dinner. And when we landed, I swore I'd never fly again.

I stumbled into the ladies room at the terminal, where I also had been deposited, and there was Montez, sitting on a small cot, looking worse than some patients I'd seen right after they died. She asked, "Did it happen to you, too?"

It seemed like it would have been obvious, but I tried to keep myself under control. "Yes! It happened to me and I'm not going to ever let that man forget it!"

I was sick. I was mad. And I was determined to get even with that half-wit, irresponsible show-off someday, somehow, someway.

The pilot carefully arranged it so that the next passenger would not be aware of the condition of her predecessor. One after another, the innocent young nurses were put through a dangerous, foolhardy, frightening introduction to flying. One after one, they came to earth sick as a dog. And all the while, he was laughing himself to death, having a ball. Some people have an odd sense of humor; a sick sense of humor. The rest of the nurses and I, who had been subjected to that idiot's cruel practical joke, harbored ill feelings of the first magnitude and planned to get our revenge, but fate intervened.

A few months later, this daredevil took one too many risks. He lost control of his plane during a dangerous stunt. He crashed and was killed.

We were sorry he lost his life being such a daredevil show-off, but we counted our blessings that we had landed safely after being the helpless victims of one of his wild escapades.

His needless death was a great grief to his father, who was such a kind, respected doctor, a stable pillar of the community, a man everybody loved and admired, a man who had given his son every advantage. His father's whole life was dedicated to saving life, with a strong belief in the preciousness of this God-given gift. And it makes you wonder what happened to cause his son to turn out the way he did, with so little regard for human life, both his and the lives of others.

Chapter 13
THE PROFESSIONAL MOURNER

Part of the pleasure of nursing is the wide variety of experience, because all cases are different and I had some dillies, but one that topped them all put me in the role of a 'professional mourner.' Later I learned that there have been professional mourners throughout history; people hired by the family of the deceased to dress in black, or other appropriate clothing of the period, to go through the motions of moaning and groaning to exhibit signs of grief on behalf of the deceased's family.

In ancient times, the public mourners would even put on sack cloth and spread ashes over themselves as part of their paid performance. As I understand it, the professional mourner was engaged to provide comfort to the grieving family and show the community that the departed was worthy of recognition. It was a status thing.

My job as a professional mourner was mainly to provide comfort to the family. No moaning and groaning. No sack cloth and ashes. It merely took me out of my nurse's uniform into my regular street clothes.

The occasion was the funeral of a man whose childless widow was in very poor health. Her husband had died suddenly of a heart attack and her nieces and nephews were afraid the trauma of the service might be too much for her own weak heart. My job was to see her through the funeral activities. The nursing care administrator called and gave me my instructions. It was not an ordinary assignment.

She said, "Miss Perkins, I want you to dress in a nice Sunday outfit and go incognito to a funeral tomorrow." I was intrigued, feeling that I was being sent in a little late in the game. I tried hard not to be cocky as I asked, "What do you want me to do at the funeral of a person I don't know and one who is surely beyond my skills as a nurse?"

Overlooking my impertinence, she explained. Before the service, I was to report to the widow's oldest nephew at the funeral parlor. He was to introduce me to his grieving aunt and I was to stick with her like glue until after the interment to be sure she survived.

"You are to stay beside her constantly. Be sure you have nitroglycerin tables with you and an extra hanky. You will sit beside Mrs. Jones (not her real name) in the area reserved for the family. Pat her hand occasionally and let her know by your actions that you care for her and sympathize with her loss, but don't you dare let her know you're a nurse. That would only upset her more."

As a nurse, I had had some strange duties to perform, but this won top prize.

The administrator continued, "You are to give Mrs. Jones plenty of attention and sympathy. And try to look perky to lift her spirits." Off the top of her head, she said, "If you have a hat with a feather in it, wear it!" She completed her instructions: "You are to go home with Mrs. Jones after the interment and eat a bite. Give her plenty of attention and be sure she is all right before you leave. You will be paid private duty wages for one shift. Good luck!"

The next day, I went to the funeral home wearing the recommended hat, complete with feather, a very long feather. I made my way through a room full of relatives and friends talking in muted tones. I found Mrs. Jones' nephew and introduced myself. David (not his real name) was a tall, nice-looking brown-haired man, with a slim build; a man somewhere in his mid fifties. His face was haggard, with the weight of his responsibility. He looked like he needed a little handholding himself.

Mrs. Jones turned out to be the dearest little lady in her eighties, with beautifully coiffured white hair, deep blue eyes, and a serene expression on her wrinkle-free face; giving an overall appearance that she had been well cared for all her life. One good look convinced me she had been given a sedative by a caring physician to help her through the day. Her nephew introduced us.

"Aunt Augusta, this is Miss Perkins. She has come to be with us during the funeral."

Aunt Augusta acknowledged me in a gracious manner. "It is so kind of you to be with us." No questions were asked. No further explanation was given. And from then on, I became her shadow.

During the service in the chapel, David sat on one side of his aunt and I sat on the other. From time to time, I patted her on the hand and tried to comfort her. I rode beside her from the funeral parlor to the cemetery. I sat beside her during the interment, patted her hand and commented on the beauty of the handsome floral casket cover, a mass of deep red roses, which must have cost a fortune. I sat beside her in the car going home, patted her hand some more and talked about how beautiful the day was and how fortunate we were that it hadn't rained. I sat beside her during the small family get-together in her elegant home in one of the city's fine old residential sections. I patted her hand some more and enjoyed an excellent repast. A well groomed, uniformed maid came by with a large sterling silver tray, offering delicate crystal glasses of red wine, but I declined.

By and by, the guests started to leave and since Mrs. Jones seemed to be accepting her husband's death with marked composure, I felt it was safe for me to go. As I said goodbye to her, she took my hand in hers and looked up at me. "My dear, you have been so good to me. Would you mind telling me who you are?"

I felt that the sedative and I had both done our jobs efficiently, so I confessed. "Mrs. Jones, your nieces and nephews were concerned about you and they arranged for me to come be with you to be sure you were all right." I paused a moment. "I'm a nurse, Mrs. Jones."

She smiled and looked at me with those blue eyes. "Well, I thought you were a very pretty young lady and very nice, but I had no idea who you were. I thought you were a part of the undertaker's staff."

I took my leave as graciously as I could, with my punctured pride. I didn't think I looked like an undertaker's assistant. I'm not exactly sure just what I thought an undertaker's assistant should look like, but I was confident I couldn't have looked like that. After all, I had done what the nursing administrator had suggested. I wore a tailored black suit, which I thought most appropriate, and with it, an elegant black hat, with a beautiful feather in it; a very long, perky feather. I was sure I looked like a fashion model and much more glamorous than any undertaker's assistant could possibly have been. My hat had such a stunning, long, perky, curly-cue feather!

Chapter 14

NOSTALGIA

My last summer at South Highland, I had a couple of weeks vacation and went to Vernon to visit my family. I still remember how strange it felt. I knew I was still a part of the family, but an intangible remoteness made me feel I had grown apart from my parents. I had heard older nurses talk about this experience. They said, you'll go back to visit, but it'll never be the same, because you've learned to be independent. You've learned how to live your own life and make your own decisions. You'll keep on loving your folks and wanting to do things with them and for them, but it'll never be the same again.

During those days at home, I made a couple of dresses and helped Mama can some tomatoes. Daddy seemed in such good health, none of us dreamed that his time with us was going to be so short.

I enjoyed long walks to some of my old favorite haunts. One took me to the old swimming hole, nestled in a grove of trees on the edge of town; the scene of many happy times. The water hole was fed by Yellow Creek. It was a puny waterway, but strong enough to make its way by Turner's Mill and the pond. As I approached the pond, I heard happy shouts, high-pitched squeals of laughter and saw a bunch of youngsters romping around, jumping up and down and disappearing under the murky water and popping up like playful seals. It reminded me of the times I used to take Lema and Elvin there on hot summer days and I noticed the present crowd did like we used to do on occasion. We'd change into our swimsuits at the swimming hole. A big clump of bushes served as a dressing area, even though some of the girls thought it didn't provide enough privacy. The boys teased them and called them sissies and said there were other things to think about, like things that live in the water. Swimming in such natural surroundings was risky, but to my knowledge, no one was ever bitten by a snake, although there were occasional stings from wasps and bees. And there was one case of poison ivy that was funny to everybody, but Elvin.

On that day, Elvin had an errand to run, so he said he'd bring his swimsuit and meet us at the pond. When he arrived, he noticed the most popular dressing area was full of cast off clothing and towels, so he went to another clump of bushes to change. Unfortunately, the thicket was full of poison ivy, which went unnoticed in Elvin's excitement of going swimming, plus the daring act of dressing on the scene, since a little girl he took a shine to was among us. Poor Elvin. He had the fairest-skinned in the family and was allergic to everything.

Elvin made the mistake of leaving his jeans pulled wrong side out on top of a bush graced with the poison ivy and while he whooped it up in the pond, the poison infiltrated his jeans and within a few hours after dressing, Elvin started feeling uncomfortable, and the itch became worse and worse until poor Elvin was practically like a Mexican jumping bean. We tried not to laugh, but not very hard, and Mama made him a special buttermilk and baking soda lotion to ease the situation, but it was several days before Elvin started acting normal. And it was a long time before he joined us at the swimming hole again.

During my meanderings, one day I walked past the old highschool building, which was rich in many happy recollections and a few heartaches, like the time I ran away to Birmingham and caused so much pain to a lot of folks, including myself. I remembered the fun times of all the athletic events: being a cheerleader or playing on the team; the heart-breaking disappointment of losing and the unabashed exhilaration of winning.

A flood of memories rose from my growing-up years. The parties held at my home and the happy confusion of getting decorations up for special occasions. The preparation of food for every get together. The excitement of getting a new dress. Dancing to a marvelous record player at the home of a friend, one of the very few who owned such an expensive means of sound reproduction. Prom parties in the spring and summer that made you feel like you were practically grown up, because you were allowed to walk to the end of the block after dark with your prom partner, even if he was a dud. Jolting, joy-filled hay rides in the fall. Nighttime wiener roasts over orange-red fires outside somebody's house, or in a forest clearing; laughing and joking, watching the red sparks dance upward and disappear; backing away from the glowing logs when they got too hot; waiting for the wieners to cook to perfection and tasting better than any two dollar steak. Afterwards, the marshmallow roast; watching the white confection turn brown; sometimes seeing it become charcoal coated and grabbing the sweetness from the stick, quick, before it had a chance to fall off. Then telling ghost stories, while somebody built up the fire to ward off any nearby evil spirits or wild creatures, which might be lurking just on the other side of the darkness.

I remembered the fun of trick and treating on Halloween and some of the bad things we did, like scattering ashes on the porches of a few self-centered folks, who didn't have a nibble to share with a bunch of enthusiastic ghosties and goblins. We shouldn't have done that.

I remembered the happiness of sharing holidays in the lean times and the fabulous feasts of Thanksgiving and Christmas in the good times, when the whole house took on the intoxicating aroma of the turkey roasting in the oven and the mouth-watering smell of the cornbread dressing baking with celery and onions; the colorful display of foods on the holiday table; deep orange pumpkin pie, green beans cooked with ham hock, dark red cranberry sauce, luscious sweet potatoes baked with brown sugar and topped with pecans and golden brown marshmallows.

Preparations for Christmas started weeks in advance of the happy festive day, with a lot of scurrying around trying to decide what we'd make for which person, when it was too costly for store-bought gifts; pulling the old decorations from the attic, including the little clay ornaments Mama helped us make when we were growing up; brisk excursions into groves on the outskirts of town to help ourselves to a fine tree and draping it with silver icicles and tinsel and colored construction paper chains.

The last Christmas I lived at home, we had the luxury of electricity and the tree came to life and blossomed with glowing multi-colored lights shaped like Santas, fish, trees, cars and animals, angels, and a radiant silver star for the highest tip of the tree that went all the way to the ceiling; family treasures that were carefully stored and used year after year.

Random thoughts rushed through my mind: the joy of buying a new Easter outfit; the pleasure of getting a new pair of shoes, especially white canvas keds, which were used for all kinds of sport activities. We didn't have to have a different pair of shoes for each sport like folks do nowadays. There were times if we got one new pair, that was something special and I remember the tug at the heart and the disappointment, when the family budget didn't allow even that.

When times were rough, Lema, Elvin and I were expected to pitch in and help with the family responsibilities, doing extra chores at home when Mama had to work outside the home. And when we were old enough, we went out into the workaday world and got employment. One of my first jobs was folding papers at the Lamar Democrat. Daddy was always kind of quiet when things weren't going well, but Mama was never at a loss for words. She always reminded us how much better off we were than a lot of people. And if there was something we wanted and the prospects looked bleak, one of her favorite sayings was: "If there's not a way; find a way!" And she didn't mean for the goal to be accomplished any way other than honorably. Living by the Golden Rule was paramount.

When I was growing up, Vernon was a dry county. So, supposedly, there wasn't too much opportunity for backsliding and wild living. But I remember the talk about bootleggers hiding out in the country. The bootleggers made 'whitelightning,' which Granddaddy Perkins called the work of the devil. There were a few citizens who quietly made beer on their back porches, but we did not engage in this activity. Mama didn't even make blueberry wine, which was considered on a slightly higher plane. Out of respect for the Lord and preacher Granddaddy Perkins, our house was bone dry. But I have happy memories of the whole family helping make great sorghum syrup, when the ribbon cane was harvested. We stripped off the hard exterior and cut it so it would fit in a big iron pot. And when it was all done, we'd take hot biscuits and bore a hole in the middle and fill them with that sweet-tasting liquid for lunch; maybe for an afternoon snack; or with sausage and eggs for the best breakfast in the world.

The memories I have of the years with my family are fond ones. Some yank at the heartstrings and bring a tear to the eye and a lump in the throat; some bring a poignant smile and others can still produce a good belly laugh.

Growing up in Vernon was not a bad way to go.

Chapter 15
THE REWARDS OF BEING A NURSE

One of the most rewarding aspects of life is being able to look back on the work you have done and feel that it was worthwhile, that it meant something to your fellow man and thereby brought satisfaction to you, along with whatever monetary benefit it might have provided. That's the way I felt about nursing. Today, I look back on the years I spent as a nurse with a sense of satisfaction, knowing I did what I was supposed to do at that particular time in my life and did it despite the daily heartache of coping with pain and deadly disease.

Daily, I lived with the knowledge of the terrible diseases which could afflict people. The great horror was the diagnosis of cancer and anyone of any age could be susceptible. In your daily rounds, you could meet some nice man, woman, or child for the first time, look on the chart and know they would probably die soon, and you hoped your eyes wouldn't betray you as you braced yourself to stand by them in the short, or long, hard battle ahead. I'm sure nurses today feel much the same way about AIDS. Today cancer cures provide some hope. In the 1930's there was little that could be done. Sometimes this tenacious virus took a long time to take its final devastating toll, and it made your heart bleed to watch the gradual deterioration of a human being, no matter what age. The lucky ones went quickly. Others would make a little progress and be allowed to go home for a while, but when they left, you always knew they would be back; time and again, until the end. And when the end came, you could only feel a sense of relief for the deceased and the grieving family. The patient no longer suffered and you knew time would ease the pain of loved ones left behind.

I think it was the eyes of the patients that really got to me. The look of trust and belief that the doctors and nurses could cure them, no matter what was wrong. The look of hope in the beginning. The questioning, wondering gaze, when the outcome was uncertain. The look of fear, no matter how hard they tried to hide it. The unnatural sparkle in eyes, induced by drugs to ease the pain. The glazed eyes of those who no longer cared. The peaceful eyes of those who accepted that death was near. And finally, the open sightless stare of eyes already looking into another dimension.

I remember Grandmother Perkins talking about people dying and she would use the expression, "So and so was blessedly released" today, or whenever. She always spoke of death as a release, a release from all the worldly cares, the heartaches, the disappointments, the dreams that are never realized, the pain. She believed we should try to accept the fact that there are many things worse than dying. She believed the good Lord doesn't want his children to suffer, and even if a life is cut short, or never has a chance to get started, as with a little baby, we should remember that God in his infinite mercy has a plan for all his children, a plan that continues for those who are released from this life.

And if you start thinking about a person missing all the happiness of living, she used to tell me that there is a joy and bliss in the heavenly life that will make this existence pale in comparison. This is the glory which awaits us, when we enter into eternity, a glory we are unable to comprehend on earth. She also suggested that it would be best not to get into a heavy discussion with The Preacher (her husband) about the following, but she believed that this glory awaits all people, of all faiths, who do like the old prophet Micah said: "Do justice, love kindness and walk humbly with your God." She and The Preacher may've had a few disagreements. Mighty few married people get by in this life without them, and Grandmother was just as stubborn in her beliefs as he was. However, most of the time, they did manage to be in accord, which made life a lot nicer. For example, they agreed that a lot of time, people blame God, when they shouldn't be doing that.

Many times, I've heard The Preacher say, "We know that evil exists. We see it around us every day. But we don't know why it exists. We are also incapable of understanding the suffering we're subjected to in this life, but we should not point the finger at God for things he didn't do. For example, there are some folks who say if God is all powerful, why does he allow bad things to happen, especially to good people; people who haven't done a thing to harm anybody. These folks don't stop to consider there are certain natural laws which don't change, and God has given free-will to all mankind. So, if a storm comes along and blows away your home, are you going to blame God? If a germ is floating through the air and you catch it, are you going to say, "God, you did this to me!" Or, if a loony guy comes along and puts a bullet through your leg, or worse still, if he kills you or somebody else, should the blame rest on the Almighty? Those who think God caused the misery feel that it's God's responsibility to cure it. Some people seem to want miracles everyday. Well, if the extraordinary became ordinary, it would no longer be a miracle, would it?"

The Preacher used to say, "There are mysteries in this life that we are incapable of understanding, and if we are presumptuous enough to think we ought to know everything, then we're trying to put ourselves on a par with God Almighty. And that's not being smart. It's blasphemy!" I thought The Preacher was a wise old owl, even if he did fly the coop sometimes on Sundays and eat fried chicken with members of his church, while his wife took care of their eight children. Granddaddy Perkins didn't preach near as much hellfire and damnation as most of the other preachers.

Mostly, he just said, "Love one another." And I tried to love my patients, especially when the going got rough.

It's hard to believe that when I first left home, I didn't really want to be a nurse. I had the crazy idea I wanted to be a basketball coach. As time went by and I survived this calling, I began to feel that God had led me into nursing. You hear talk about preachers getting the 'call'. It's my opinion a lot of people feel a 'pull' within themselves, which leads them into certain fields of service. I also believe, like Granddaddy Perkins, that you don't have to be a preacher to serve the Lord, because when you serve your fellowmen, you're really serving Him.

Well, I've fed them and watered them and bathed them and nursed them. I've given them enemas and rubdowns and shots in the arm and shots in the bottom. I've held them in my arms when they cried and held their hands while they died and loved them and tried within the best of my ability to help them get well, and I wouldn't trade a minute of it. Not the heartaches or headaches or insults or tears, or grief, or joy, or laughter or the indescribable thrill of seeing a crisis pass and a sick one healed. And although not everything in my life has worked out the way I hoped it would, or thought it could, if I hadn't become a nurse, I could never have been an airline stewardess and if I had never been a stewardess, I would never have met Dick.

And for this, dear Lord, I thank you.

Chapter 16

GREENER PASTURES ARE NOT ALWAYS ON THE GROUND

After graduation, four years of my life were devoted to nursing and I liked what I was doing, but underneath it all there was something like an itch you can't get rid of. That itch was to fly and it wouldn't go away. Even though I had a rotten introduction to flying, I still wanted to get into the business, and being a nurse made it possible. It was common knowledge that the airlines had started hiring young women nurses to serve as stewardesses. (It was unheard of at the time for a man to be a nurse. That was strictly woman's work.)

You might want to think that the concept of nurses being flight attendants was an altruistic one and maybe there was an underlying thought in this direction, but it was also a very fine public relations vehicle. Commercial air flight was still new and people were generally nervous about flying. People would literally get sick with fear. Upchucking was common and other nervous reactions could take many forms, including hyperventilating, palpitations, getting drunk and the like. It simply made good business sense to let passengers and their loved ones on the ground know that those flying were being well cared for. It helped ticket sales.

Several of my friends at South Highland had the same itch and we talked about it and read the newspaper looking for ads for nurses to join the airlines. And we dreamed.

Then one day, I read that Delta would be interviewing nurses at the Tutwiler Hotel in Birmingham. I decided to "go for it", and everything seemed to fall in place.

My first interview was with Laura Wizark, who was hired from American Airlines to select and train Delta's first stewardesses. When I walked into the room and saw her, I thought she was very glamorous. She was blonde. She was beautiful. And she was from Boston. She was a couple of years older than I, and I thought she was very sophisticated and mature and I tried to show her the proper respect due an older person. I dabbed away little beads of perspiration as inconspicuously as possible and tried to appear calm and collected. I knew I wanted to be an airline stewardess, but I never believed in cow-towing to anybody, if I could help it.

The interview progressed smoothly. She asked, "Why do you want to be a stewardess?"

I told her the truth. I had fallen head over heals in love with the idea of flying. It seemed to me to be one of the most glamorous jobs a young woman could do. And at the same time it would utilize my knowledge of nursing to which I had devoted all of my adult life. "Miss, Wizark, I've been a nurse for four years and I want to expand my horizons."

She smiled and interrupted. "You'll certainly get a chance to do that with flying."

That early in the acquaintance, I didn't feel like I had a good read on her. I didn't know whether she was pulling my leg, was taking me to be a small town nurse without any brains, or whether she was just trying to make conversation and be friendly. I decided to let it pass, but wanted her to know that flying wasn't my only option. "I have an opportunity to go with the Veterans Administration. I can go to the University of Chicago and finish my formal education, or be a stewardess." I hesitated a moment, grinned and leveled with her. "Being a stewardess sounds more exciting!"

I had always heard that people from Boston were cold and reserved, kind of snooty, but Miss Wizark started to thaw.

"Being a stewardess is a thrilling job and so far as the other positions are concerned, going with the Veterans Administration sounds a little dull and as for going to college, you've already had the benefit of comparable college training in learning the subjects required to become a registered nurse. And with Delta, You'll be continuing your education. You'll be building on the experience you've already acquired."

My thoughts exactly.

"You'll actually be a nurse in the air, except hopefully you won't have many sick patients. You'll meet exciting people in all walks of life.

You'll literally walk on air. You'll work in the air! And although your head may be in the clouds sometimes with all the excitement, your feet will be firmly on the ground. And you'll literally be getting in on the ground floor, because Delta has never had stewardesses before. You'll be a pioneer in the airline business!" By the time Miss Wizark reached the high point of this spiel, she was waxing warm with enthusiasm and I was enchanted. She told me her plans to hire ten stewardesses. She wanted them to be well read, knowledgeable about current events the traveling public would be talking about, so the stewardesses could carry on an intelligent conversation. She asked, "Do you like sports and do you keep up with the activities of the Atlanta Crackers and the other teams?" Well, when she latched on to sports, she was getting into a subject dear to my heart. With undue modesty, I replied, "I think I can handle that subject, especially baseball." I started throwing out some statistics about the different teams and all the players and just as I was getting worked up to tell her about all the gossip and predictions for the top teams, she changed the subject. I frankly don't think she knew very much about baseball.

She wanted to know something about my present job and I told her I was the Assistant Night Supervisor of South Highland Infirmary. "It's a hundred and fifty bed hospital and its nurses training program is the best."

We talked on for close to an hour, while she told me how wonderful Delta was and I told her how wonderful I was and I watched while she made a notation about red hair and green eyes. She closed the interview telling me I'd hear from her in a couple of weeks. I got up to leave and said, "I don't believe we've talked about salary."

"Oh, starting salary is a hundred and ten a month."

That did it!

I was making sixty dollars a month working six days a week, twelve hours a day, or night as the case may be. And being a stewardess, I'd even get days off during the week. As the chance to almost double my salary sunk in, I was jubilant.

My friend, Inez Jackson, and I both met with Laura Wizark. Both of us received an invitation to go to Atlanta for a second interview. We had arranged to get an interview with American Airlines and as luck would have it, the appointment with American came up on the same day we were to go to Delta. So Inez and I flew to

Atlanta in the morning, had our interview with Delta and flew back to Birmingham for our interview with American Airlines that same afternoon. It was a super exciting day.

My second Delta interview was with Pat Higgins, Vice President in charge of operations. Mr. Higgins was a friendly man of Irish descent, not the least bit scary and we hit it off right away. He gave me a cordial welcome, which did a lot to ease my nerves and the interview which followed was about as brief and informal as it could be.

"Miss Perkins, do you think you would like the job?"

"Yes, sir! I know I would!"

He looked over my application and in a few minutes he said, "Well, I guess that sews it up. Miss Wizark will be making her final choices soon and we'll expect to see you when she gets her school set up." He walked me to the door. He gave me a big smile and a hearty handshake and said, "If you want the job, I'm sure we'll see you again." I learned later that Mr. Higgins was brand new in the art of interviewing prospective stewardesses, but I thought he did just fine. He made me feel welcome.

Inez got the same warm reception and when we left, we both felt that we had been hired, even though we didn't have a firm offer.

That afternoon, back in Birmingham at the Tutwiler, we were interviewed by Newt Wilson, an American Airlines representative and were both offered a job. Mr. Wilson was very nice, but he was also insistent that we give him an immediate answer whether yes or no. Our instructions were to send him a night letter to reach him the next day at the Reid House in Chattanooga. (Nowadays, you'd simply send a fax or e-mail.)

I liked Mr. Wilson and all the things he had to say about American Airlines and I felt very torn. The necessity to respond immediately added a tremendous stress, because after ten P.M., I shared the full responsibility of the hospital with my supervisor. I helped run the hospital, including the O.B. (obstetrics) patients and emergency surgery and the switchboard. They believed in diversification at South Highland.

At that time, I was not only carrying a heavy load at the hospital, I was concerned about my mother. My father had passed away recently from a heart attack and I knew she needed me badly. American had told me I would be based in New

York for six months and would not be able to come home, so just before the deadline, I made my decision.

I chose Delta. So did Inez.

Birdie Bomar & Kathryn Bankston

PART TWO

The following pictures are only a few of the many intended for this book, pictures which are presently inaccessible since Birdie's move from her home of so many years.

BIRDIE'S VERY YOUNG PARENTS: JOHN WESLEY PERKINS AND CLARA SANDERS PERKINS

**FRONT COVER PICTURE OF BIRDIE IN HER
FIRST DELTA UNIFORM, WHICH SHE CAN STILL
WEAR. BIRDIE DONATED THIS UNIFORM TO
THE DELTA MUSEUM AT THE ATLANTA
AIRPORT.**

A HIGHSCHOOL PORTRAIT OF BIRDIE.

BIRDIE WITH HER BROTHER ELVIN G. PERKINS
(LEFT) AND HER COUSIN J. M. MCCARVER IN
FRONT OF HER CHILDHOOD HOME IN VERNON,
ALABAMA

DELTA PASSENGER PLANE, SHIP 42. EARLY 1940'S. THIS IS THE DC-2, WHICH MADE THE MAIDEN FLIGHT WITH DELTA'S FIRST STEWARDESSES. (PLEASE NOTE THIS IS NOT THE ACTUAL PLANE.)

**DICK BOMAR AND HIS COUSIN MARY LOUISE,
AFTER A JOYRIDE IN DICK'S PLANE IN THE
LATE 1930'S.**

**CAPTAIN DICK BOMAR IN HIS EASTERN PILOT
UNIFORM.**

**JULY 25, 1942. HAMI.TON & LIBBY TODD &
RICHARD & BIRDIE BOMAR ON THEIR
WEDDING DAY AT COLLEGE PARK METHODIST
CHURCH.**

**DICK AND BIRDIE, LEFT, SOCIALIZING WITH
AN UNIDENTIFIED COUPLE.**

**DICK BOMAR BEING COMMENDED BY EDDIE
RICKENBACKER WORLD WAR ONE HERO AND
PRESIDENT OF EASTERN AIRLINES. THIS
PICTURE WAS TAKEN AT THE END OF DICK'S
LONG ORDEAL IN THE HEALING OF HIS HAND.**

**C. E. WOOLMAN, FORMER PRESIDENT OF
DELTA, DISPLAYING A TROPHY OF THE DELTA
DC-2, TO FIVE OF DELTA'S FIRST STEW-
ARDESSES. L-R, SYBLE PEACOCK, LAURA
WIZARK WHO TRAINED THE FIRST
STEWARDESS CLASS OF TEN, LAJUANA
GILMORE MCBRIDE, BIRDIE AND INEZ
JACKSON.**

BIRDIE WITH JOY MALONE, WIFE OF BILL MALONE, A FORMER OUT STANDING EASTERN PILOT. PICTURE TAKEN AT ONE OF THE RETIRED EASTERN AIRLINES PILOT'S ASSN. MEETINGS

BIRDIE AT A MEETiNG OF THE R.E.A.P.A., Retired Easter Airlines Pilots Association. BIRDIE SERVED AS PRESIDENT OF THIS AUXILLARY OF THE PILOTS' WIVES.

**A SOCIAL AFFAIR SPONSORED BY THE
EASTERN PILOTS' WIVES ASSN. L-R,
UNIDENTIFIED MEMBER, BIRDIE BOMAR, ANN
VANCE AND LILLIE HURT.**

**BIRDIE, FAR RIGHT, IN WHITE PANTS SUIT,
DURING ONE OF THE TOURS SHE GAVE AT
DELTA'S SHOWING THE DC-2.**

**A CHRISTMAS CARD TYPE SNOWY SCENE OF
BIRDIE AND DICK'S HOME OVERLOOKING
NISKEY LAKE IN ATLANTA, GEORGIA.**

BIRDIE STANDING ON THE DOCK IN FRONT OF HER HOME ON NISKEY LAKE IN WARMER WEATHER.

Birdie Bomar & Kathryn Bankston

**A RECENT PICTURE OF BIRDIE WEARING HER
ORIGINAL DELTA UNIFORM POSED BESIDE AN
OLD DELTA 'STEWARDESSES WANTED' POSTER
DURING A DELTA CELEBRATION.**

Chapter 17

THE FIRST DELTA STEWARDESSES

Everything seemed strange and new and exciting when I came to Atlanta to start my job with Delta, February 26, 1940.We interchanged roommates so many times, I can't remember all the transitions, but I would like to give recognition to the other girls, who became Delta's first stewardesses. I know Miss Wizark had planned to have ten girls in the class, but one evidently fell by the wayside. My eight remaining classmates were: Beth Clark; Lajuana Gilmore, who was my counterpart flying from Fort Worth to Atlanta the first day Delta put stewardesses on their flights; Inez Jackson, who had come over from Birmingham with me for our first Delta contacts; Vernell Jones, Ann Kelly, Eva Parrish, Syble Peacock, and Ellen Sappington.

The first few days, I stayed in a room at the Hangar Hotel with three other stewardesses. When the dust settled, I moved into a two-bedroom apartment over the Hangar Restaurant. This was shared with four other girls. Each bedroom had two double beds, which meant there was one girl too many under ordinary circumstances, but all five were never there at the same time, so things worked out fairly well.

It was the scene of considerable activity and served its purpose. In addition, it provided a bonus feature we could have done without. We got a continuing blast of odors wafting up from the hotel kitchen: the distinctive fragrance of stale grease, stale coffee, grilled hamburgers and fried fish, and various and sundry other smells, which are hard to take anytime of the day or night, but especially first thing in the morning. A third move elevated my standard of living to a one-bedroom jewel with a kitchen, where my roommates and I could create our own aromas, when time allowed. Two other girls shared this unit with me.

In 1940, stewardesses were the only women hired by the airlines, other than the secretaries, and we became spoiled with the flattering attention we got from the men. This suited us just fine. The men in the ground crews were actually a little nicer than the pilots, who had their noses slightly out of joint about females being added to the flightcrew.

They had serious reservations about the merit of this new policy and it showed. For example, when we went on flights, the name of the stewardess was posted on a metal strip at the front of the plane. Since all of us were nurses, an R.N. (for registered nurse) was placed after our name and some wiseacre pilot came up with the idea that it stood for "Run & Nag." They couldn't help teasing and generally the verbal jabs were a 'put-down', implying male superiority. But, basically, the pilots were good to us.

Delta was good to us, too, but there was blatant discrimination against stewardesses in all the airlines at the time. You couldn't be married. You couldn't weigh over a hundred and ten. You couldn't be over twenty-six years old and you couldn't socialize with the pilots. There was some fudging on all these restrictions, with the possible exception of your weight. If you stepped on a scale, the truth came out. If you got caught breaking the rules, your future was in jeopardy. The airline was particularly picky about no socializing between pilots and stewardesses and to cope with this, when there was an overnight stay, at the end of the line, they parted. In Fort Worth, which was the end of the line for my regular flight, the pilots were stationed in the Worth Hotel and the stewardesses were placed in the Blackstone Hotel. Delta's president, Mr. Woolman, was a 'father figure'. He wanted Delta to be known as a 'family organization' where high moral and ethical standards were not only expected, but demanded.

In fairness to all concerned, a footnote should be added here. Being associated with the airlines turned out to be a happy hunting ground for marriage partners for lots of young men and women with healthy hormones and honorable intentions. My husband and I were a prime example with our own private merger between Delta and Eastern. I'll share this glorious happening with you shortly.

Training to become a stewardess was a snap in comparison with the grueling three-year preparation required to become a registered nurse. It took two weeks to complete our course of instruction set up by Laura Wizark.

We were taken through the DC-2 and taught the different parts of the plane. During this exciting period, on dates, we took our boyfriends to the hangar and explained the things we'd learned about the elevators, the flaps, the exits, the storage area for baggage and the mail pouches and sometimes we'd give them a peek at the mysterious instrument panel. Then we'd go into a prolonged discussion of meteorology and get them to quiz us about the different types of clouds, so we could be knowledgeable if the sky was telling us a storm was pending.

Since I have always liked stormy weather when the sky is filled with dark billowing clouds and lightning darts across the sky and the world is filled with mighty claps of thunder, I got a special kick out of learning about Saint Elmo's fire: static electricity that produces a stunning glow of fire caused by atmospheric conditions; it is fire often seen around the propeller tips and the windshield of the aircraft. It can sometimes build up into a large glowing ball of fire on the nose of the plane and get the pilot's attention with a jolting, loud noise through his radio headset. And before we had pressurized cabins, pilots told me they'd seen it discharge and roll down the aisle like a fiery orange basketball. In pressurized cabins, it will build up on the nose of the plane and remain until the temperature changes. I thought it was beautiful and exciting every time I saw it, even if it lasted only a few seconds.

From the beginning, Delta wanted it's stewardesses to be alert to the customer's needs. Customers were to be pampered, catered to and pleased. Customers were always right. Customers could do no wrong. If a customer was rude to you; you were not rude in return. If the customer pinched you on the bottom, you were not told to turn the other cheek, but you were not allowed to reciprocate. We were taught how to keep our balance in planes not as smooth and steady as the ones we have today, while dispensing box lunches and coffee, conversation and encouragement; how to be charming and provide magazines, pillows or whatever else was needed to keep the customer happy. We were provided with well-equipped first aid kits and advised to keep an alert eye for the immediate need of burp cups. Hiring registered nurses to serve as cabin attendants was a practical move on the part of the airlines. It was like killing two birds with one stone. They had the advantage of attractive young women to serve meals and make the passengers feel comfortable. They had the advantage of an available marketing tool to make the wives of the traveling executives feel that their husbands would be well cared for. It made everyone flying feel a little more secure, knowing there was professional nursing assistance immediately available. I could see how the expertise of a nurse could be put to good use in this line of work, but basically, it was a whole new world.

Delta also wanted its stewardesses to look smart. With this goal in mind, Miss Wizark sent us to Rich's, considered by many to be the finest department store in Atlanta at the time. We had our hair styled in the glamorous setting of Rich's Beauty Salon and purchased our specially designed uniforms in Ladies Clothing. We bought our good-looking navy outfits for fall and winter from Rich's. Later, we bought a spring and summer beige uniform from Neiman Marcus, in Texas. We were smart-looking all right, but the financial burden was staggering. Delta expected us to pay for our uniforms. They were exactly the same amount as our monthly salary: $110. Every season, I had to buy a new uniform and my budget was in a constant state of shock.

Chapter 18
AN INAUGURAL FLIGHT WHICH DIDN'T FLY

The two-week training period required to become a Delta stewardess was fun and exciting. Everybody was all hyped up in anticipation of the big inaugural flight scheduled for March fifteenth. Miss Wizark announced that there would be two flights: one from Atlanta going west to Fort Worth and one leaving Fort Worth heading east to Atlanta. Departure time for both flights was 10:00 A.M.

One stewardess would be selected for each flight. We all hoped we might be chosen. It was a prestige thing. Everybody tried to be nice about it saying things like: "I bet you'll get to go." Or, "It really doesn't make that much difference to me." I didn't say a word; I just waited and tried to believe I was prepared. As I recall, a couple of days ahead of the designated fights, Miss Wizark made the announcement.

LaJuan Gilmore and I were the lucky ones. And for about forty-eight hours, the excitement built up with both of us thinking that March 15, 1940 was going to be one of the most wonderful days we would ever experience.

When the fifteenth came, I still couldn't believe it was happening, but there I was running across the tarmac, feeling on top of the world, til suddenly I spotted a figure coming toward me at full speed and immediately, I knew it meant trouble. The trouble approached in the usually lithe and lovely form of my boss, Miss Wizark. As she approached, I noticed that she had lost her customary composure as she raised her voice and told me what I already knew.

"Miss Perkins! You're late!"

She didn't stop to lecture. She kept going in her direction and I kept going in mine and scampered up the steps into the DC-2 as fast as my legs would carry me. I was fifteen minutes late, but the plane wasn't due to leave for forty-five minutes. Generally, Miss Wizark was calm and under control. I'm sure she was hyped-up over this progressive first interchange flight between

Atlanta and Fort Worth with her brand new charges. I could understand this, because I was so nervous and excited, I was about to take flight without the plane.

March 15, 1940 was a beautiful breezy, sun-filled morning. A red letter day for Delta. A brilliant red letter day for me, too, because this was a maiden flight and I was one of the maidens.

These historic interchange DC-2 flights were set to depart Atlanta and Fort Worth at the same time; twelve passengers were to be delivered to their respective destinations and mail pouches were to be exchanged in Jackson, Mississippi. This was an important part of the mission, because delivering the mail helped to pay the bills.

Inside the plane, I soon realized that I was functioning better than it was, which meant that things didn't look too promising. Miss Wizark, Delta's Chief Stewardess, came back on board. She paused to ask why I had been late.

As a rule, I am gifted about coming up with an appropriate excuse. I didn't want to tell her that in my excitement, I had dilly-dallied around and had no excuse. I floundered and said simply, "I'm sorry. I goofed." I cast my eyes down and tried to look humble. It didn't come easy.

She admonished, "Don't let it happen again."

As soon as I relaxed enough to look at the folks onboard, I realized I was not her only cause for concern. Mr. C. E. Woolman, the tall, dark-haired founder and president of Delta, was talking with the two pilots: Captain George Sheely and Co-pilot Jack Roth. Nobody was smiling.

I remained in the background and waited for something to happen. Miss Wizark talked with the men, while I checked on the coffee and box lunches to be served during the flight. Time passed and I wondered why they weren't letting the passengers board.

About fifteen minutes before the scheduled take-off, an unhappy "mother-in-law" appeared. He addressed Mr. Woolman.

"Sorry, boss. There can't be a flight today. We have a mechanical failure. Something's wrong with the engines. They're not warming. We'll have to postpone the trip til tomorrow."

Mr. Sanford was a nice guy. He was chief pilot with American Airlines, which sold the Douglas DC-2's to Delta. As the "mother-in-law", it was his responsibility to be sure everything was functioning properly, mainly the plane and the pilots. And if he was a little bossy at times, like mothers-in-law are accused of being, he carried a big load and I guess he was justified.

As soon as he received the bad news, Mr. Woolman took charge. He turned to the chief pilot. "Set it up for the same time tomorrow." He spoke to Larry Campbell, the radio operator, who had been standing by. "Contact Fort Worth and let the other folks know the interchange flights will run to-morrow instead of today."

Slowly and silently, we filed out of the plane. The red-letter day had fizzled.

And we weren't the only ones with problems. We found out shortly that the Fort Worth flight had also gone belly-up when the Texas plane got bogged down in a bunch of red tape, courtesy of the Civil Aeronautics Authority.

It looked like the Lord didn't intend this interchange flight to launch on the Ides of March.

* * * * * * *

The next morning, I reported to work fifteen minutes early. I wore my snazzy new navy-colored uniform with its matching hat cocked on one side of my head and was sure I exuded an aura of confidence, if you didn't look too closely. The problem was chronic. I was sweating. Every time I get nervous or excited, I sweat.

It was a great day, just cold enough to make it invigorating, but I was so invigorated, beads of perspiration covered my brow and I dabbed away with a handkerchief as I hurried along. Heading for the plane, I looked up at that large mechanical bird with a sense of pride, because I was a part of an exciting airline and felt lucky I had been chosen for this flight marking the beginning of Delta's "cabin attendants."

I was wrapped up in my own thoughts, when two dispatchers ran toward me. Alex Rainouard and Bill Bradley dashed on either side and quickly pulled me through the door of the dispatch department. They were all worked up, shouting that they had to talk with me. We were good friends, but I didn't like being dragged into the place where they weighed cargo. They knew I was getting ready to take-off on my first flight. I was nervous. Who wouldn't be? First day on the job. They should've known better.

I yelled, "Hey! What's going on?"

They sat me down on the nearest chair and Alex spouted, "Something great has just happened! Birdie, you're gonna remember this day! You're gonna be Number One in seniority! You're gonna be Miss Wizarks' first 'fly girl'!"

Bill broke in; "We've just found out that the Fort Worth flight has been delayed, so you'll be the first Delta stewardess in the air!" They were so happy about my unexpected and unearned small status, I hated to be a wet blanket, but I needed to get on the plane.

I popped up and said snappily, "I could care less! I'm just glad I'm going!"

Alex called after me. "You may not care now, but you will later on. Mark my words, Birdie!" And with shouts of "so long" and "good luck" following me, I boarded the plane.

Everybody was there as planned. Mr. Woolman displayed his million-dollar smile. The beautiful Miss Wizark looked pleased and tried to ignore my sweat problem. The pilots, who had years of experience flying, tried to be pleasant in the midst of all the to-do, even though they had doubts about how the addition of women to the crew was going to work out. The mechanics and the "mother-in-law" pronounced the plane operable. Co-pilot Roth said the mailbags were secured. The passengers boarded. At ten o'clock sharp, the door closed and we taxied down the runway for take-off.

Delta was proud of its large, new DC-2's, which could carry fourteen passengers, lined up seven on each side by the windows. There were other airlines, which had already started using stewardesses, but Delta was proud of its move in this direction. It was proud, too, of this new grasshopper service, with stops in Birmingham, Meridian, Jackson, Shreveport and Dallas. A lot of hard work had gone into the preparation of this inaugural flight.

Delta had pulled out all the stops with a big publicity promotion and the problems of the day before had inconvenienced a lot of people. It meant rescheduling arrangements with the newspaper reporters, photographers and mayors of the cities where we stopped along the way. I'm sure there were a lot of unhappy people, particularly the mayors, but they recognized the potential revenue this new service could bring to their communities and they appeared the next day, with big smiles and large bouquets.

Although they were late getting started, the same activities were planned for the eastbound flight. My counterpart, LaJuan Gilmore, was late getting in the air, but at least she didn't have our boss and the president of the company to cope with.

I was a nervous wreck and it was so obvious, Miss Wizark made an intelligent and compassionate decision, which earned my undying gratitude. She decided that I would do better without her, so she deplaned at Shreveport and from then on, I loosened up and started feeling like the star of the show, as I dispensed coffee, food and optimistic conversation to the passengers. Never mind the fact that the president of the company was also on board and had something to do with all this. By the time we approached Fort Worth, my enthusiasm and self-esteem soared to heights I had never known before.

When we landed, I made my way through the small boisterous crowd and had my picture taken with the mayor and Mr. Woolman and received another lovely bouquet of flowers.

Inside the terminal, a lot of people were milling around and somebody dragged me over to get a publicity shot made with a tall, lanky guy parading around with a stuffed steer. I'm not sure what he was promoting and in the confusion, at first I didn't realize who I was standing next to, 'til I turned and looked up into the handsome, smiling face of a very young Jimmy Stewart.

He was the actor, but I was the one with stars in my eyes and that night, my feet never touched the ground. I felt like I could keep right on flying on my own little cloud, filled with the wonder of how my life had turned in this direction.

Chapter 19
THE 'GLAMOUR' OF IT ALL

Remember Icarus? He was the guy in Greek mythology who thought he could fly like a bird. His papa built beautiful waxwings for the two of them to escape from prison, but his construction job was not well thought out. Icarus flew too close to the sun; the waxwings melted and Icarus fell into eternity. Icarus was one of the early ones to give flying a bad reputation.

Some people today still get unsettled with they look down from an airplane window and consider the distance between them and the earth and they would just as soon not get any closer to the sun. But I don't think folks today get as edgy about invading the air rights of the birds as they used to. In the early 1940s, commercial flight was still fairly new; the novelty of it produced a goodly share of up-tight passengers and this fear of flying created a lot of ways to keep a flight attendant in constant motion.

Not long after my inaugural flight, I met my first real challenge; the first of many to follow. It helped me develop clearer understanding why Delta insisted that its stewardesses be registered nurses, because we surely needed the nurse's experience of discipline in order to survive. It helped to have a little milk of human compassion. And a sense of humor was a godsend.

I watched the various reactions to the stress of flying with interest. Some got very quiet and buried their heads in a book or magazine and tried to ignore the circumstances. A huckster might exhibit his zeal to get to the top of the corporate ladder, busying himself with reports for his client. Some sensibly passed the time taking a nap and sleep, whether pretended or not, was always beneficial, particularly for the stewardess.

Then there were the tipplers. The airline didn't serve alcohol and the passengers weren't supposed to bring it onboard, but some did. I found the surreptitious tipplers the most interesting, and unfortunately, often the loudest and most offensive. Coats and pillows were lifted in strange ways, as the traveler pulled out a small flask and took a swig. Some bent over, as if looking for something on the floor, while taking a swallow. And some made their way back to the restrooms with such frequency, you wondered if they had a bladder problem. One way or another, the "secret activity" became obvious, as the volume of speech increased, sprinkled with vulgarities directed at the stewardess. Sometimes the inebriated traveler started telling raw jokes in such a loud voice, it was difficult for the close-by passengers to escape them.

A trip which comes to mind was a regular grasshopper flight from Atlanta to Fort Worth. It was a popular flight with businessmen and it was rare to have women or children. When we pulled out of the Atlanta airport, there were only a couple of vacant seats. We expected one passenger to board in Birmingham and another in Jackson. Among those on board were several men from Georgia, heading for a cattle convention in Fort Worth. A couple of Texans were returning to Dallas. A small boy, about eight years old, the minimum flying age for a child alone, was going to visit his grandparents on a farm out from Fort Worth. One executive was going to Birmingham for a business meeting.

The sun was splashing all over everywhere and everybody was in high spirits as we took off. And then the fun began.

One man toward the front of the plane started drinking in earnest as soon as the wheels left the ground and began displaying his vulgar vocabulary of words decent people found offensive. After warning him to keep his foul language to himself, I went back to check on our littlest passenger. Thank goodness, he was in the rear of the plane out of earshot from the idiot, who was making such a fool of himself. Jeremy was a nice little boy. (Jeremy and all other names used in this chapter are not the actual ones.) This was his first flight and he was scared; trying valiantly not to show it. I tried to pay some attention to him from time to time.

"Jeremy, tell me about your grandparents' farm."

"It's big." Jeremy was not much on talking.

"And what does your grandfather grow?", thinking in terms of my father's modest farm.

"He grows cattle. But, mostly, he has oil wells."

"That's nice," I said, seeing dollar marks all over the place. "Look out the window. You might see some interesting sights and I'll be back to check on you in a few minutes. Would you like a cold drink?"

"Yes'm," he said softly.

I went to the front of the cabin chatting with the passengers, asking the standard questions: "Is everything all right?" "Would you like a magazine?" "Is this your first flight?" I ignored the man who had been spouting off earlier.

One of the men returning to Dallas was a real dude; a giant of a man. He looked to be at least six-four, with sharp blue eyes, nondescript graying hair at the temples and a ten gallon hat, which he refused to remove. His height and hat made him so tall, it annoyed a finicky small man in back of him. One of my responsibilities was to try to keep everybody happy, so as nicely as I could, I requested the removal of the Stetson. He mumbled a muted oath. He was not revolting like the man with the garbage mouth. He smiled a lot and tried to exhibit what he thought was a winning personality; one that was sure to knock the ladies dead, and since I was the only female on the flight, I didn't think it presumptuous to suppose that he was trying to charm me. I was not impressed. He made no effort to conceal the sterling silver flask, which he pulled from his pocket, and you would have had to be blind not to see the multi-carat diamond ring he wore. It was so big, it was vulgar. He tried to be jovial, but he overplayed it.

"Mam, you sure are a pretty filly. How'd you like to live in Dallas?"

I tried to be pleasant. "I'm happy living in Atlanta, thank you." I changed the subject to the business at hand. "I'll be serving coffee in a few minutes. Would you like a cup?"

He grinned and winked at me. "I sure would, mam."

As I moved to the next passenger, I felt a decided pinch on my bottom. I looked back at him in anger and saw him turn his head toward the window with a sly smile on his face. He mumbled, "I could use a little extra sugar, too."

I was furious, but held my temper and went on.

The men going to the cattle convention were reasonably well behaved. Their conversation was about the problems of raising cattle, the high price of feed and the constant worry about disease. "Gentlemen, I'm serving coffee. Would you like some?" Almost in unison they responded, "Yes, mam!"

After serving coffee and checking on the little boy, I went to the pilot. He said we were on schedule and should landing in Birmingham within half an hour. In Birmingham, we deplaned one passenger and boarded a lovely lady. It wasn't often we had a woman traveling with us and I looked forward to having another member of my sex on board. In talking with her, I found that her trip was a sad one. She was going to Dallas to visit her brother, who was dying of cancer.

Under less stressful circumstances, she must have been a very attractive woman. She was middle-aged, of medium height, a little on the heavy side and walked with a slight limp. She had black hair streaked with gray and the deepest cornflower blue eyes I've ever seen. She was fashionably groomed in good taste in a navy blue suit, a neat white blouse with a conservative navy straw hat. Mrs. Haroldson was not feeling well. She was distressed over the critical condition of her brother and she looked a little green around the gills. She had developed a migraine headache, a queasy stomach and her physical problems were compounded by her fear of flying. She had appealed to me when she first boarded.

"My dear, I'm feeling ill and I need you to help me get through this trip." My nursing nature rose to the fore.

I assured her. "Mrs. Haroldson, don't you worry about a thing. I'm here to help you." I walked her to her seat. "I think you'll be more comfortable if you take off your hat and let me tilt back your seat as far as it'll go. Just close your eyes and rest and I'll get a couple of aspirin and a cold cloth to put on your throat."

It was obvious she was miserable. Her subdued moans were audible. I spent most of the rest of the trip going back and forth from the lavatory to put fresh, cold cloths on her throat to stem what seemed an inevitable inner tide.

It erupted when we were about to land in Dallas.

Following the Federal Aviation Commission regulation, I put her seat in an upright position, and as she approached the ninety degree angle, out it came in the most amazing display of projectile vomiting I have ever seen. Like a water hose that is suddenly turned on to full strength, the undigested contents of her troubled stomach went all over my hair, my face, my lovely new uniform, and in an instant, I was a disaster. What's more, I stank!

It was terrible.

Mrs. Haroldson felt very bad about it. I felt even worse! But, what could I say? According to company policy, the customer is always right.

As I stood there in shock, with a good portion of Mrs. Haroldson all over me, across the aisle, the

Stetson Texan, who had put his mark on me earlier, jumped up and shouted, "God almighty!" He pulled out a huge handkerchief for me to wipe my face. "I always thought you fillies had a glamour-type job. But, God damn, mam. You can have it!" I'm sure he was relieved that he had not been in the line of fire.

I cleaned off the worst of the damage and the plane landed without further incident.

Just before we landed at Fort Worth, I went to the back of the plane to check on Jeremy, our young traveler from Atlanta. As I leaned over to assist him with a couple of small bags, he looked up solemnly and said, "Miss, you don't smell so good."

I ignored the evaluation and tried to be nice.

"Jeremy, you're a fine traveler. I hope you have a good time visiting your folks on the farm. And, remember, always fly Delta!"

The nose is supposed to lose its sense of smell, or at least part of it, when exposed to an odor for for a while, but there was no escaping my smellyness.

It was bad. It cut into my social life. I became an outcast. The exiting passengers turned their heads when I tried to say goodbye as they filed past me. The rest of the crew outright shunned me.

I was painfully aware of the truth of Jeremy's candor and so was everybody else.

I left the plane with the captain, taking for granted that I would ride into town with him and the rest of the crew. The captain was brief.

"Sorry, kiddo. You can't ride with us. You smell too bad."

I had already been told that. I knew I smelled bad, very bad, but I was cut to the quick. The captain was abandoning a member of his crew.

He did, however, make arrangements for me to take a taxi to the hotel. The driver never said a word, but he did let down his window. The company dutifully paid for me to get my hair washed and styled at one of the nice beauty salons in Fort Worth and picked up the tab for my uniform to be cleaned and deodorized.

That was a long time ago, and I still flinch when I think of this episode with Mrs. Haroldson.

I think I could write a book on the 'use and abuse of the Delta stewardess uniform'. And I thought the uniforms were so beautiful. I gave my first navy outfit to Delta for its archives. I had held on to it just like girls save their wedding gowns. That uniform had served me well and endured many insults. Another time it was put to the test happened on a lovely summer day in the early period before Delta moved its headquarters from Monroe, Louisiana, to Atlanta. And I will now use real names.

Mr. Leigh (pronounced "Lay") Parker, a Delta V.P. had told me a number of times he wanted me to meet his wife. Mr. Parker was a regular traveler on my flights to and from Monroe and Atlanta. He was the guest speaker at many meetings, where he promoted Delta and I understand he was a good one, but it took a toll on his digestive track and we got acquainted mainly because Mr. Parker relied on me to provide Bisodol to calm his nervous stomach before making a speech.

The above information is provided as an introduction to the occasion when I finally got to meet the lovely Mrs. Parker.

Mr. Parker was not on this particular flight. Mr. Parker was the furtherest thing from my mind. I was mainly concerned with a beautiful young flaming-red-haired passenger and her infant son, whose active kidneys had depleted his large diaper supply. This was before the days of mass marketed disposable diapers and the young mother turned to me to handle the situation.

"I hear you do wash," she said as she blithely handed me a plastic bag full of dirty diapers.

With the lesson thoroughly impressed in my brain that we must please the customer, I automatically replied, "Oh, yes, mam," and held my tongue, although there were choice words I wanted to say. It wasn't as if I had nothing else to do but wash diapers. We had a full ship. I had to serve coffee and a meal to the passengers. I thought, "Oh, Lord, how am I going to cope with this?"

I hurried back to the one bathroom on the plane and started to wash the soiled diapers. The weather became unsettled, producing rough vertical currents. There were several dramatic drops in altitude and I knew I had better see to the passengers. I was right. Almost everybody had started getting sick at the stomach. They would have gotten sick a lot sooner, if they'd been doing my laundry job. I began dashing throughout the plane handing burp cups to those who couldn't get to the one bathroom; cleaning up the overflow; trying to take care of my duties, washing some kid's smelly dirty diapers and sharing the bathroom every few minutes when I heard a frantic knock at the door.

It was not a good day. And I was a mess.

By the time we landed, I was sweating clear down to my waist. My hair was a wreck and the

Delta hat, which was supposed to give a glamorous, dashing appearance cocked on one side of the head, was a dangling, pitiful creation, which would have sent the designer into immediate shock.

I consoled myself with the thought that in all the commotion, I didn't have to serve and clean up after a meal. No one wanted to eat.

I was exhausted. I took care of my paperwork and was deplaning in Atlanta, when I suddenly saw Mr. Parker coming toward me with his beautiful wife. She was looking fresh and neat and lovely as a spring daffodil and I hated her. There I stood, exposed, with no means of escape.

Mr. Parker looked surprised. He shouted, "Birdie, what on earth has happened to you? You look a mess! For months, I've been telling my wife what a great gal you are and finally, I've brought her to meet you and you look like a tramp!" Mr. Parker was shocked out of his fine sense of diplomacy and I didn't fare so well myself.

This was the final insult. I was hot. I was tired. I was embarrassed. I was irritated beyond words, but not quite, and I let him have it.

I yelled, "If you'd been washing diapers and trying to cope with a ship full of sick folks, you wouldn't look so good either!" and stormed off with scarcely a glance at the dewy fresh Mrs. Parker.

Later, under more pleasant circumstances, I met his wife again and we became friends. I found her to be a very compassionate soul.

So much for the glamour of being a stewardess.

Chapter 20
FLIGHT AMONG THE STARS

When I had my first interview with Laura Wizark, she told me I would meet some interesting people on the job, and she was right. There were times when I was literally walking among the stars and prominent people in other walks of life. I remember one particular trip. It was my regular grasshopper flight from Atlanta to Fort Worth. July 4, 1941.

One of the passengers was Eugene Talmadge, Georgia's colorful "Gov'nuh", who was flying to Birminham for speech-making and barbecue. He was in a jolly frame of mind. I guess he was going over to give support to his fellow Democrats in his neighbor state. I remember we had our picture taken together in the Birmingham Airport and he was in his famous red suspenders. Governor Talmadge stood there leaning back with his thumbs pulling out his suspenders, with a big political grin on his face. He thanked me for the ride, just like I had been the pilot and paid me a lot of nice compliments. He may have been in Alabama for the moment, but he didn't forget that I was one of his constituents. He was a good politician. He also taught his son to be a good politician and later Herman Talmadge became Georgia's governor.

Another prominent passenger on this flight was the beautiful actress, Ava Gardner. She was on her way to Dallas, where she would take an American flight to the West Coast. Enroute to Dallas, we stopped at Shreveport and boarded Mr. H. B. Hunt, who was probably the richest man in America at the time. He was a regular passenger with Delta going back and forth from Shreveport to Dallas. On this flight he had his son with him, a young man somewhere in his twenties. They whiled away the time talking with each other about business. Miss Gardner was alone and just before we got into Dallas, she called me and said, "I'm just miserable. I have this long wait ahead of me in Dallas before the American flight leaves and I don't know what to do. I don't know anybody. I don't know the city and I was wondering if you might have any suggestions."

I looked at Mr. Hunt sitting a couple of seats in front. I knew he always had a big barbecue on the fourth of July and I decided to take the bull by the horns. I approached him and said, "Mr. Hunt, I'll bet if you knew I was all alone and lonely in Dallas and didn't know anybody and didn't know what to do for several hours between planes, I bet you'd invite me out to your place for barbecue."

His face lighted up and he said, "Miss Birdie, you just come right along with us. We'll feed you the best barbecue in the world and I'll have somebody bring you back to the airport." I said, "Mr. Hunt, I can't go, but there's somebody I'd like for you invite." For a second, he looked like he was sorry he had been so cordial until I said, "Turn around. See that lovely lady back there? That's the famous actress, Ava Gardner. She's all alone and lonely and has a long wait until the American plane takes off late this afternoon." Well, when Mr. Hunt and his son turned around and saw the beautiful raven-haired Ava, they both lit up like a couple of Roman candles and when Miss Gardner realized who had given her an invitation, she put out some sparks of her own and when they deplaned, they were all smiles. They seemed pleased with each other's company.

Several weeks later, Miss Gardner sent me a note thanking me for a wonderful time. That was nice. A lot of people are not that thoughtful.

Besides the Hollywood celebrities, there were always a bunch of politicians flying here and there hopefully taking care of important political matters. They were always around, but there was one special flight I'll always remember, because it ended up with my having a great vacation while on the job.

The reason for the trip was a sad one, but when you're working for an airline flying all the time, you can't afford to go to pieces about the tragedy of other planes going down. A congressional committee came from Washington to investigate an Eastern crash in Vero Beach, Florida. The folks from Washington included Congressman Klayberg from Texas, Congressman Nicholson from Oklahoma and "Big Jane" (not her real name) a court reporter. I'll never forget her. She must have been a good two heads taller than I was. From Delta, there was Captain George Cushing, a former VP with Eastern; Co-pilot George Monogold and I was the stewardess. It was a charter plane, a little Lockheed 10, which was a good plane, but it was so low, you had to bend over to get in and once you were on the inside, you couldn't stand up. But, it got us there and back.

In the meantime, while the congressional committee of two and a Federal Aeronautical Association representative put on hip boots and went out gathering evidence in the snake-infested marshes, I walked the golf course or walked the beach and everybody got together for happy hour and dinner in the evening. This idyllic state continued about a week, until the congressmen had to fly to Miami for further investigation of Eastern. They wanted me to go with them, but Captain Cushing put his foot down. "No dice! She works for Delta, not Eastern!"

I guess one of the biggest thrills I had in meeting celebrities was when I flew with Sir Laurence Olivier and his wife Vivien Leigh, (who won an Oscar for her role as Scarlett O' Hara) on a hair-raising charter flight from Nashville to Augusta. At the outset, I must tell you that Augusta was not our initial destination. We were suppose to land in Atlanta, but the weather was just about as bad as any I encountered during my flying career. Pure pea soup, or more like black bean soup, because it was dark and forbidding.

Now, I happen to like flying in bad weather. I find it exhilarating, but not everybody feels this way. Sir Laurence was one who didn't share my enthusiasm.

The purpose of this trip was to promote a bond selling tour tied in with a second premiere for "Gone With The Wind", the classic movie about the old South. Sir Laurence was very gracious about the commitment. His wife was not and soon gave the impression she felt that attending a second premiere of "Gone With The Wind" was about as stimulating as a stale martini.

Also on board was the famous director of suspense films, Alfred Hitchcock. With his background, you would imagine that he would be comfortable with the zero-zero weather, but with due respect to the dead, Mr. Hitchcock ate and drank so much, he was in a chronic state of dyspepsia and he kept his nose buried in a script, except for the times he was calling me for an antacid, which was frequent. Miss Leigh's hairdresser was also on board, but she never said a word and slept most of the time.

Since this was a newsworthy event, the Atlanta papers had sent two reporters to cover the story: Marie "Veezy" Scott representing the morning Atlanta Constitution and Ernest Rogers, with the afternoon Atlanta Journal. I imagine both of these fine, experienced reporters felt that they had been on other assignments equally as exciting and they settled back with their own conversation.

The morning of the great adventure, Captain Dolson, Co-captain Nelson, the reporters and I had flown from Atlanta to Nashville, with the intention of bringing back our famous cargo to Atlanta for all the festivities, but this was not to be. It became a painful re-play of my very first flight with Delta, which never got off the ground. The dependable, popular Lockheed ten-passenger charter plane was ready and waiting and waiting and waiting, while the American Air Lines plane, which was to deliver the stars to us, faced zero visibility and the inability to make the trip for two days. Trying to make the best of a bad situation, the pilots, reporters and I went to the Hermitage Hotel to wait for the weather to improve. There wasn't a lot to do in Nashville and the weather didn't help, but we were able to gather together each night for a good meal in the dining room, listening to the music of Frances Craig.

In defense of Miss Leigh's sour disposition, she had been through a rough time and I guess some of her attitude was understandable.

After we got a clearance to take off, the weather went from bad to worse. An attention-getting electrical storm arose displaying plenty of fireworks. The plane wobbled and Miss Leigh sat in her seat with her hands in the praying position and, I suppose, in order to keep her mind off all the negative weather, she started bossing Sir Laurence and kept it up the whole trip, telling him: "Larry, do be quiet." "Darling, read this." "Laurence, we are not going to crash." "Dear, there's no need to go to pieces." And with all this encouragement, Sir Laurence became slowly unglued. He kept moaning and saying, "My God! We're going to crash!" "Miss Perkins, do you think we're going to make it?" "How does the pilot know which way to go? "My God! I'm scared!"

Amid the roaring storm outside and the hysteria inside, the pilot called me to the cockpit and yelled, "Do anything! Do whatever you have to! Draw him a picture! Get him calmed down!"

So I drew him a picture.

The plane was not steady in its course and neither was I. I stumbled down the aisle with paper and pencil and with a sudden, slight drop in altitude, I almost landed in his lap. I gained my composure, knelt down beside Sir Laurence and drew him a picture.

It was not the finest example of graphic art, but it helped to explain a navigational system which is no longer used. I told him, "Just as you have certain signs to identify which way you're going when you're traveling on the ground, you also have signs to guide you in flight. We have navigational airways with beacons placed approximately every ten miles along the way. These are a guide for the pilot. Whenever he sees these, he knows he's on course. And if you'll look out the window, when you see these flashing, rotating lights, you'll know we're going in the right direction." Then I prayed that the lights would be working and that he'd see them.

My prayers were answered! A few minutes later, through all the black turbulence of the storm, a small glittering signal was seen. When he first glimpsed the lights, with an amazing amount of gusto, in his crisp English manner, he shouted, "Efficiency! That's what I like! People who know what they're doing!"

It's a blessing Sir Laurence had the lights to look at, because just before we were to land in Atlanta for the big shindig, we learned that Atlanta was weathered-in.

We couldn't land.

Considering that this was a repeat performance for the entertainers who weren't able to land in Nashville for two days, the Delta officials were understandably concerned that the whole group might engage in some high-voltage histrionics.

Delta Flight Control contacted the pilot by radio and instructed him to go to our alternate landing point in Augusta. A few minutes later, in the midst of thunder and lightning, Mr. Oscar Burgstrom, assistant to Mr. Leigh Parker, called to give instructions regarding the care and feeding of the dignitaries.

I hated to break the news that there would be no landing in Atlanta. There would be no participation in the festivities. We were heading for the Forest Hills Hotel in Augusta. Mr. Burgstrom was concerned about bad public relations with the prominent guests and told me, "Give them anything they want!

Mr. Hitchcock was the first to take advantage of the offer. He said, "I'll take fifteen bottles of liquor!"

We landed in Augusta, had a good night's sleep and the next morning, we were on our way to Atlanta after all the fun, festivities, disappointments and frustrations were a memory. Everybody seemed a little subdued and Mr. Hitchcock snored softly and slept with little smile on his face all the way back to Atlanta.

Miss Leigh was pleasant to me, but she was still mad at the world in general and at the inconvenience to which she had been subjected in particular. She had only one thing on her mind. She wanted to get back to England. She wanted to get away from this whole bloody mess. A delayed reaction blossomed suddenly from all the trauma she had experienced and she was the one who became hysterical. Sir Laurence, who was now the picture of self control, calmed her down and assured her that she would see their beloved England again soon. Thank God they didn't both become unglued at the same time.

Just before we landed, Miss Leigh gave me a box of beautiful orchids, which someone had given her before the beginning of this unscheduled, unsettling comedy of errors.

There is an epilogue to this event. For Delta's fiftieth anniversary celebration, I wrote Sir Laurence and invited him to come as an honor guest to the festivities. I received a prompt, courteous reply in which he told me he could not come, but sent congratulations and thanked me for helping him through a stormy journey so many years ago. It was a lovely letter. I have it tucked among my things somewhere.

When I told this story to a friend, she asked, "Do you think he really remembered after all those years?"

I told her, "No one could have forgotten that trip."

Chapter 21
THE AFTERMATH OF NOVACAIN

The Hangar Restaurant with the kitchen odor which penetrated the environs of my temporary apartment has gone the way of all things, still the restaurant is dear to my heart because it's where one of the most important events of my life took place.

It wasn't a glamorous place, but what the Hangar Restaurant lacked in glamour, it more than made up for in convenience. The hotel was close to the airport and a lot of the airline personnel went to the restaurant for food, drink and comraderie. Employees of the airline lived there; mostly the unmarried pilots and stewardesses. It countered the restrictions the airlines imposed on the pilots and stewardesses about not staying in the same hotel on overnight trips. Nobody worried about it.

The restaurant stayed open from early in the morning until midnight for those who were traveling and the airline personnel felt comfortable there.

The day which ultimately changed the course of my life started out soggy and got worse. It was dull, gray, depressing, and I had a dental appointment. I have never considered a trip to the dentist to be fun, no matter how nice he might be. To make it easier, I borrowed a car, which belonged to my roommate's boyfriend.

After the dentist had done his thing, I headed back to the airfield with a sore jaw to return the car. A thin veil of rain covered the world. It did nothing to lift my spirits. I decided to stop by the Hangar Restaurant for a cup of hot coffee and, hopefully, some lighthearted conversation.

Outside the entry of the hotel, usually, there was a black man sitting by a bale of hay. I guess this was supposed to give a touch of the late 1850's atmosphere for travelers. His name was Franey (pronounced Frah-ny), but he looked like everybody's idea of Uncle Remus, so that's what we called him and he didn't seem to mind. Franey's job was to assist people coming into the hotel, or restaurant; helping with their luggage or parking their car. His age was unknown. He had some years on him, but not enough to keep him from being spry. His bald head was fringed with hair like white lamb's wool and most of the time his shiny, dark round face wore a smile. He was pleasant to everybody. Everybody knew Franey. Everybody liked him. And Franey liked his well-earned tips.

When I drove up, Franey ran toward me with his big, black umbrella to help me in out of the rain, and in my haste, which has always seemed to be my normal state of activity, I forgot to put up the window of the car all the way. Unaware of my carelessness, I entered the restaurant. It was during the mid-afternoon slow period and I didn't see anybody I knew; just a couple off in a corner, who looked like they didn't need any extra company, and there was some guy sitting by himself on a stool at the lunch counter. I decided it was a case of any port in a storm and sallied up to the counter and sat beside the stranger. At that point, all I wanted was a cup of hot coffee to ward off a cold from the miserable weather and somebody to help me forget the recent assault on my mouth and the general indignity of going to the dentist.

The man at the counter and I had progressed to the stage where I knew his name was Dick and he knew my name was Birdie, when Uncle Remus came dripping in, grinning, and announced, "Miss Birdie, "Ah done rolled up de glass on yo cah."

I said, "Thanks, Uncle Remus," and gave him a dime.

Franey bobbed up and down with his enormous smile and said, "Thank ya, mam," and turned to Dick. "I rolled up de glass on yo cah, too, suh!"

My new acquaintance just sat there and said, "Thank you, "not even turning around. Maybe he was going to give Franey a tip and had slow reflexes. The delay provoked a sense of indignation which put my natural state of cockiness into gear. I said, "Give him a dime, you cheapskate!" Dick didn't say a word. He just gave me a side long glance as he reached into his back pocket and brought out a dime for Franey.

Up until the time he turned around, I hadn't paid too much attention to what he looked like, but when I did, I liked what I saw. Matter of fact, I liked it very much. He was a tall, slender man, about six feet. And his eyes; they were a soft blue and showed no sign of resentment at my rudeness. They kind of smiled at me. Nice, compassionate eyes. Bedroom eyes, I thought. They reminded me of the actor, Charles Boyer, and for a moment, I regretted that I had been so cocky. The feeling didn't last, because he warmed up and we started talking in earnest, just like people do when they meet someone they like instantly, or almost instantly, and we just kept talking until about an hour later, we had a date lined up for that evening. And I forgot about my sore mouth.

Our glamorous first date took us driving down Stewart Avenue to a drive-in, where we had a coke and got acquainted. I found out that Dick had just arrived in Atlanta from Spartanburg, South Carolina, where he had worked on the ground crew with Eastern. He'd recently gotten his flying status and was transferred to Atlanta. The fact that Eastern and Delta were rivals didn't bother either of us. There was a lot of fraternizing between the two airlines and Dick and I fraternized quite nicely together.

I wasn't dating anyone particularly and so far as I knew, Dick wasn't tied up with anyone else, so we started making a pair. We dated regularly, but I kept a few irons in the fire, just in case. There was a lawyer in Fort Worth and occasionally, there would be others who took me out to dinner or to the movies, but Dick rapidly became my steady guy. If he kept any extra irons in the fire, I never knew it.

You couldn't call our courtship a whirlwind affair. It lasted two years and we had great times together without a commitment. Dick and I were both outgoing people and a lot of the time, we partied with other young couples. We went to the movies, to some of the inexpensive eateries and every once in a while, we piled a bunch of friends in the car and went roller skating at the Lakewood Rink, not far away from the airport. We didn't have much money to spend. Dick made two hundred dollars a month and I brought home a hundred and ten. This did not sustain a lot of riotous living even with the price of things back then, but we had fun.

After we started feeling sure of each other, Dick announced one day he'd like to take me to meet his parents. Not long after that, we got an invitation to drive up to Bell Buckle, Tennessee, population five hundred. Bell Buckle derived its name from an American Indian name. It was a charming community and had more cultural influence than you'd ordinarily find in a town its size. It was the home of Webb Academy, a fine prep school, where a lot of the financially comfortable parents from all over the southeast used to send their children; a lot of the graduates went to Vanderbilt Medical College. Dick had gone to Webb and had the credits to graduate, but just before graduation day, he had an opportunity to learn how to fly and he took it.

That first trip to Bell Buckle almost got both of us in a barrel of trouble and I'm mostly to blame. I guess I could put the blame on Dick, because he had such a magnetic personality. I just couldn't help cuddling. Since Dick was driving, he was limited as to how far over to the right he could lean. So I was practically in his lap, snuggled up and thinking nobody was paying any attention to my reaching over and giving him a few buzzes on the cheek and a nibble or two on the ear. I was decidedly in a compromising position, when we passed through Calhoun, Georgia, which wasn't much bigger than Bell Buckle. Calhoun was almost a case of: now you see it, now you don't; it was so small.

Everything seemed lovely. We were laughing and talking, oblivious to anything else, when suddenly from behind a clump of evergreens, a cop darted out and started tailing us, flashing the light on his car. He didn't have to go fast, because Dick was driving well within the speed limit, and we wondered what on earth we'd done.

Dick was worried. He said, "I wonder what's up."

I said, "That cop was just waiting for somebody to come along, so he could write another ticket!"

Dick pulled over to the side of the road. From the minute I laid eyes on that man, I didn't like him. He got out of the car and ambled over in a leisurely self-assured manner. His pot belly looked like it would pop through his wrinkled uniform. He propped against the side of the car, bent down to get a good look at us through the open window and tipped back his hat. He was obviously smug about making another arrest for the day; he knew he had us. He spat a squirt of tobacco on the side of the road and in a country nasal twang informed us, "We don't do thangs in these here parts, like you and your friend been doin'."

Dick was courteous, as always. "What did I do, officer?"

"Young man, a couple of blocks back, there wuz a schoolbus approachin and you should've stopped."

"Officer, I saw that bus. It was a half a block away."

"Well, now, ah reckon it's gonna be your word against mine, ain't it? We like to take real good care of our younguns and school buses always have the right a way, even if they are a little distance from the intersection. You have to look out for them buses round here." I was repelled by his his illiterate speech, slovenly look and insulting manner.

"But, officer," Dick tried to break in. The sleazeball kept on: "Ah'm chargin you with exceedin' the speed limit, failin to stop for a school bus." He paused and gave me a lascivious wink adding, "and ah'm chargin the young lady with molestin the driver!"

I thought I would explode. Dick didn't say a word. We followed the police car in silence. Inside the courthouse, the officer said, "That'll be eighty dolluhs."

I shrieked, "Eighty dollars!"

"Eighty dolluhs, mam. Pay it, or we'd like to have both of you as our guests. There're a couple of empty rooms in back. One for each of you, but ah can't say they's real comfy."

We didn't have eighty dollars! That was almost half of Dick's salary for a month! I didn't wait for Dick to speak. In my best voice of authority, I said, "Officer, give me the phone." I decided to pull rank on him. "I'll call the Comptroller of Georgia, Lindley Camp, to handle this!" With that information under his cap, he crawfished.

He drawled, "Well, mam, ah think we can take care of this matter without bringin in iny uther folks."

I glared at this sorry specimen of humanity, who was trying to con us and didn't give an inch. The outcome was that he cut the fine to twenty-five dollars. Dick paid it and we were on our way, with me not sitting quite so close.

*   *   *   *   *   *   *

You had to be careful about Bell Buckle. If you didn't stop in time, you passed it.

We drove up to a small, neat frame house. Mr. and Mrs. Bomar were sitting on the front porch in their comfortable rocking chairs, waiting for us. Xennie (pronounced Zenny) Pickens Bomar and William Henry Bomar were a kindly couple. They had the relaxed look of people who are content with their lives. Mr. Bomar was a little shorter than his son. He owned a men's clothing store and was proud of his fine custom-made suits. You might not think a quality store like his could survive in such a small community, but the faculty and students at Webb Academy kept him in business for sixty years. Mrs. Bomar was a dear lady, cheerful as the day is long. She was a Sunday school teacher given to quoting what she thought was appropriate scripture.

She had a delicious hot dinner waiting for us when we arrived: crisp, golden fried chicken, rice steamed to perfection with every grain standing apart, corn on the cob, green beans, the daintiest little biscuits and apple pie for dessert.

Mama and Mr. Pickens, Mrs. Bomar's parents, lived in a slightly larger frame house across the street. In back of the house, Mr. Pickens had a spread of forty acres, where he raised Tennessee walking horses. Dick took me over to visit and I was enchanted. I was used to visiting my own grandparents out in the country, but feeding those beautiful animals and giving them friendly caresses was a new experience.

After a nice visit with Dick's folks, we headed back to Atlanta.

Atlanta's population was around three hundred thousand, but it didn't offer much in the way of good restaurants and entertainment places. It was coming out from under the depression and the great building and growth which followed World War Two had yet to come. But we had some great times. And when I say great times, I don't mean beddy-by times. This was way before the sexual revolution. I don't want to give the impression that there wasn't a lot of smooching going on, but it was generally thought that the heavy stuff should wait until after marriage. There were some fast girls around and occasional shockers popped up, like the rumor of a girl going down to the Georgia Tech football stadium and taking on the whole team. But, statistics show, there were a lot more virgins before marriage than there are now. It was an era of innocence and a lot of good healthy fun and I expect we were happier playing it the way we did as opposed to the promiscuity of many of the young people today, who have a different sense of values.

Things were generally lively at the Hangar Hotel. Dick had a good friend, who lived directly under my apartment. Buddy Batzel, an Eastern pilot, was the son of a Methodist preacher from Pennsylvania. He was a famous stunt man of the day, known world-wide as Bat Man.

Buddy was different. He didn't do things the way you'd expect and this was part of his charm. The first time Dick and I invited him up for dinner, we were sitting on the balcony waiting for his knock on the front door, suddenly there were two hands on the railing, followed by a head, shoulders, arms and the full body of Buddy, who had had great fun scaling up the outside of the building. From then on, with a joyous "Surprise!" this was the way he made his appearance.

Being from the north, Buddy had never discovered the true joy of black-eyed peas and cornbread. After an initial hesitancy, he became an avid fan of this southern favorite and he used to shinny up and Dick and I let him help with the preparation. Buddy used to double date with us and one evening, I tried to introduce him to a friend of mine.

I said, "Buddy, there's a real nice girl I want you to meet."

Buddy clowned around. "No, thank you. I'd rather just eat black-eyed peas and cornbread tonight."

I encouraged him. "Buddy, she's so beautiful, she could qualify for Miss America."

"No. I think I'd prefer the black-eyed peas and cornbread," he teased.

"I can solve that, Buddy. We'll ask her to come here and eat with us. If she likes the black-eyed peas and cornbread, you'll know she's a worthy candidate for your attention."

Buddy agreed. She liked black-eyed peas and cornbread. And they were eventually married. Ann Leonard was a lovely dancing teacher from

Cincinnati, who decided she wanted to be a stewardess. I trained her at Delta and thought she was something special. Buddy thought so, too. They had a long, happy union. He always said it was a "perfect marriage."

Ann passed away a few years ago.

Many times, when he would come back to Miami Shores from an Eastern flight, he would go and sit by a lake, where her ashes and the ashes of their son are scattered. After her death, Buddy wrote a lovely letter to thank me for introducing him to the love of his life.

Chapter 22
THE MAN I LOVE

I came to Atlanta in February 1940. The war had started in Europe, but there was strong talk about isolationism and not getting involved in other peoples' problems. Dick and I met a few months later in July and had a wonderful, carefree courtship for nearly two years. During this time, I learned a lot about the man who meant so much to me. He told me about growing up in Bell Buckle and his first ride in an airplane, when he was six years old. The scene of this historic event was on his grandfather's farm a few miles out in the country.

One afternoon when he and his grandfather were in the fields, they heard a plane and saw a pilot circling in an OX-5 Jenny circling overhead. They stood there fascinated at this unexpected entertainment, while the pilot performed all sorts of antics in the sky. Dick's quick eye caught it first. He yelled to his granddad, "Look out! He's going to land!" At first, Dick edged around in back of his grandfather's large overalls for protection, peeking to the side to watch the amazing event. It was a rarity in those days to see an airplane, much less watch one land right in front of you. It would be something of a surprise even today, especially if you weren't at an airfield.

The pilot gave a big grin, waved, hopped out of the small plane and walked toward them like this was an everyday occurrence. Dick's granddaddy was nice to him, like he was to everybody, but when the man asked permission to use his field to pick up passengers to take to Bell Buckle, granddaddy said, "No, sir. I don't think I want to do that."

Dick's initial apprehension was replaced by excitement over the possibility of getting to see the plane again and watch the pilot pick up paying passengers to give them a joyride around Bell Buckle. He begged.

"Granddaddy, please let 'im do it!"

Granddaddy finally agreed and the barnstormer was so pleased, he offered Granddaddy and Dick a free ride. Granddad said, "I think I'll wait til the Lord gives me wings, before I do any flyin. You can take the boy up, but," he warned, "don't you let anything happen to him."

That was in 1919. Dick was so thrilled over going up in the air and looking down at the earth, he made up his mind that one day he'd be a pilot.

At seventeen, he left Webb Academy just before graduation day and went north a few miles to Murfreesboro to take a job with the Interstate Airlines. He worked long, hard hours as a general flunky, running errands for practically no pay, but he was happy. He had made up his mind he wanted to be a pilot and it was right about this time, he had a thrilling experience for a young man who was determined to fly. He had his first cross-country flight as a passenger in the mail compartment of a Pitcairn Mailwing from Nashville to Chattanooga. I used to tease Dick and accuse him of being a stowaway.

Besides flying, Dick and I found we had another interest in common. We both liked to sing and he had a nice baritone voice. He also played the trumpet and told stories about his mother taking him once a week to Nashville for his trumpet lesson. Later on, those lessons paid off.

We loved to sing together and many a time, when we were driving along, one of us would start a song and the other would join in. And whenever

I could get to a piano, we sang together. Or, Dick would play his heart out on his trumpet. He told me about one of the first melodies he learned. He played "Kiss Me Again" for his first student recital, while his mother shed a few tears. She always said, "That was the prettiest thing I ever heard in my whole life." Mothers are like that. Dick admitted that he was proud, too.

Dick had another musical talent of lesser stature. He loved to play the jug. The jug was a porcelain bottle, which allowed him to produce an um-pah-pah bass background to a melody. It was fun, and always a big hit. At almost all the parties we hosted or attended, Dick could be counted on with either the trumpet or the jug, but he'd never tell in advance which it would be. Long after we were married, Dick learned to play the Hammond Chord Organ and I remember many a time hearing him play a few verses of "Beautiful Dreamer" at three o'clock in the morning before he left to go fly.

When the desire to become a pilot became full blown, Dick started putting every cent he could into flying lessons. His meager salary wasn't enough, so out came his trusty trumpet. He landed a job with a dance band, which gave him enough to pay for his lessons. His instructor was R. O.

Lindsey, a well-respected World War one ace, who soon discovered Dick had a good feel for the plane. After a few flights he let Dick solo. This was his first red letter day in aviation. Another one soon arrived.

With all the time he spent hanging around the airfield, he came across an opportunity to buy half interest in a Hisso-Swallow for three hundred and fifty dollars. Lindsey offered to check out the plane for him and the adventure almost ended Dick's flying career before it got started. It almost ended Dick and Ace Lindsey.

Within a few minutes after becoming airborne, they felt a lurch and a loud thump and they knew something was wrong. The plane was flying all right, but when Dick looked around, he saw the left landing gear dangling from its fitting at the fuselage. Landing with the plane in this condition would result in a crash. They might escape with their lives, but Dick knew his three hundred and fifty dollar investment would be shot. That money represented many hours work at the field and many hours playing the trumpet til the wee small hours and Dick didn't mean to give it up lightly.

Dick yelled to Lindsey, "Hold the plane steady! I'm going out there!"

Lindsey hollered, "Dick, you're a fool! Don't do it!"

Dick paid no attention. He crawled out the rear cockpit onto the wing. He saw that the bolt had fallen out of its fitting, letting the gear strut dangle. He quickly removed his belt. Locked his legs in the flying wires. Got a firm grip and slid the upper half of his body over the edge of the wing. The strong wind current played with him like he was the last leaf on a tree and he dangled along with the flopping gear.

This dare-devil feat was written up later by an Eastern Captain, Jim Webb. "He looped the belt into the wheel and began working his way back onto the wing, pulling the wheel and strut into place with his belt. He couldn't sit holding it while Lindsey landed. The weight was beginning to pull the belt from his hands. He tugged with all the strength he had; held it a moment with one hand, and thrust his fountain pen into one end of the bolt fitting.

"It held.

"With a moment's respite, Dick took a cowl wire pin from the cowling and wired the gear on securely by hooking the wire through the fitting several times. The bolt was now replaced with a strong cowl wire.

"Dick crawled back into the rear cockpit and made one of the best landings of his career without incident. The bolt was replaced for seventy-five cents."

I won't repeat what I said to him, when I heard about this incident years later. Among other things, I asked him, "What would you have done, if you hadn't had a fountain pen with you?"

He never answered. But when I finished speaking my mind, he knew how I felt and every time I think about it to this very day, I get the heebie-jeebies.

Nevertheless, Dick saved the plane. He got a lot of praise from Lindsey. The folks on the ground at the airfield had watched Dick's death defying performance and when he landed, they were clapping and carrying on, and I guess he swelled up another few inches, but I still think it was one of the most foolhardy things he ever did.

Chapter 23

HOW TO COPE WITH A FEMALE PREDATOR

One night in the Fall, after Dick had been made a pilot with Eastern, we had a date to join some friends for dinner. The weather was turning cold and it felt good to keep the car windows closed. It did not feel good when I got in the car and immediately smelled trouble! There was an exotic aroma of somebody's perfume.

It was not mine!

My nose sensed the danger of somebody trying to invade my territory and I didn't like it. For a few minutes, I didn't say anything. I tried to size up the situation. I sniffed in all directions trying to decide what the fragrance was. It was not the nice clean soap and water smell of Dick. Then it hit me! It's Tabu! The perfume of a woman on the make!

Dick looked at me sniffing the air and asked if I had a cold. I said, "No," trying not to let him see that I was rapidly approaching the boiling point. I chose what I considered a subtle approach.

"Is that a new cologne you're wearing?"

Dick laughed and confessed, "Oh, that must be the perfume of Verna Smythe (not her real name), from South Carolina. She was with me earlier this afternoon. She wants me to give her flying lessons and I drove her over to the hangar to show her around. She's a nice kid."

I thought, "Nice kid, my eye! She's out to take over my territory and even if she is a Delta stewardess, this is something I'm not going to tolerate!" I could just see her with her beautiful baby doll face, looking up at Dick with those big baby blue eyes. She was a flirt to the very core of her and was always bragging about her latest conquest. And then, after she hooked a guy, she didn't want him. The more I thought about it, the madder I got, and I knew it was time for me to learn how to fly.

In my best off hand manner, I said, "Dick, I've been thinking about learning to fly for a long time and I'd like you to teach me."

Dick acted surprised. "I thought you'd given up the idea of learning to fly."

This was a tease, although at one time, I thought it would be nice to be Delta's first female pilot. After all, I was Delta's first stewardess in the air. But, Dick and I both knew this line of thinking was too advanced for the airlines at that time.

I told him honestly, "I think it would be in my best interest." Then hastened to add, lest he suspect what I was actually thinking: "It would further my knowledge about planes. I'm sure it would make me a better stewardess." Inspiration hit and the true idea emerged. "You can give me lessons at the same time you're instructing Verna." (Meaning I can keep an eye on the two of you.) "Verna's a real swell girl," I lied, thinking if she tried to pull any fast numbers with Dick, I'd scratch out her baby blues.

Dick agreed to the arrangement. When Verna found out about it, she wasn't happy. Tough luck! There wasn't much she could do about it. Dick told her he was getting pressed for time and it would ease his busy schedule. So everything was set up for Dick to teach Verna and me together.

I was pleased with the arrangement. Dick seemed satisfied. Verna was overtly displeased.

Verna lived in a cute little duplex in Hapeville with another Delta stewardess. If she had lived in the Hangar Hotel, I could have launched a more effective campaign to discourage her from taking flying lessons from my steady boyfriend.

There were several daydreams I had about ways to get Verna out of the way. I thought I'd go to the drug store and buy some Exlax, a delightful little laxative made up in small squares to look like chocolate candy. It even tasted like chocolate candy. My plan was to transfer the cathartic to a nice white box, wrap it in gift paper, tie a lovely blue ribbon around it and give it to Verna from a "secret admirer." Everybody knew that Verna was a chocoholic, and I figured with the "gift" given the night before a lesson, it would keep Verna occupied the next day.

My next plan was to get hold of the slacks Verna always wore for our flying lessons and rip out the back seam, baste it together loosely and then at an appropriate time just before the lesson started, pull the controlling thread, like you do a sack of flour or dry dog food to open it. I figured this would get her out of the way another time.

My last daydream of revenge was really bad. I decided if all else failed, I'd somehow help Verna to trip and break her ankle or leg. I should have been ashamed of myself for having all these evil thoughts. I wasn't. Not until later.

So far as Verna was concerned, when she realized I wasn't ceding my territory, she started missing lessons. Not with any assistance from me. And not long after, she dropped out completely. Then the most terrible thing happened.

Verna started having sick spells. The doctors x-rayed her and found she had a brain tumor. She lived only a few months. And there I was left praying for God to forgive me for all my wicked scheming, wanting to get her out of the way.

* * * * * * *

I must confess I wasn't the ideal student. And I give Dick credit. He tried his best to teach me how to fly.

It was nice being together like a couple of love birds in the sky. Certainly, Dick was well qualified to teach. He had been a flight instructor before he became an Eastern pilot. The problem was not with Dick. It was with me. The trouble was my wanting to do things my way all the time.

We had discussed this earlier and it was no surprise to Dick. We had been dating long enough for him to know I was a little hard-headed. But true to his easy-going nature, he always kept calm until one particular day.

I had taken the controls of the small two-seater Taylor Craft and was having a great time feeling like a bird without a care in the world.

Dick said, "Birdie, you need to turn to the right. There's a big passenger plane behind us."

I thought he was teasing. "No!" I challenged. "I want to go this way." And I continued flying straight ahead.

This was one of the few times I ever heard Dick get really angry. He shouted, "No you're not! You're going to do it my way!" He grabbed the controls and made a sharp right turn and then I saw the big plane practically on our tail!

The atmosphere soured. Dick didn't say anything and I didn't say anything. I knew I had done wrong.

Dick flew us back to the airfield and when we landed, my knees were wobbly and I knew my future as a pilot was doomed.

On the ground, Dick turned to me in exasperation.

"Birdie! I give up! You're unteachable!" And he stormed away.

After thinking about it for a couple of days, I decided that the intense studying required to get a license was more than I wanted to tackle. I came to the wise decision that I couldn't hold down my job as a stewardess and learn to fly at the same time. I came to the even wiser decision that it might not benefit my relationship with Dick and no amount of high flying was worth putting that in jeopardy.

Chapter 24
DICK ENTERS THE AIR FORCE

Have you ever seen eagles floating high in the sky on thermal drafts? They rarely flap their wings. They float along on a current of warm air, looking like a small airplane with their outstretched wings, enjoying life without a care in the world. That's the way Dick and I were before our happy-go-lucky dream world came to an end.

From the time of Hitler's assault on Czechoslovakia and Poland, Americans were increasingly aware of the growing turmoil in Europe. Many thought the United States should not get involved. People deplored the merciless aggression. They talked about the horror of it, but after all, it was not our battle. We felt protected by the Atlantic. We felt secure in the false belief we wouldn't be brought into the conflict. And like most folks, Dick and I went on our merry way.

We worked, played, laughed and loved our way each day through a carefree courtship. We liked our work. We loved each other. We played and had fun with our friends and lived in a world removed from the reality of approaching war. In the fall of 1941, Dick expressed real concern. The Japanese bombed Pearl Harbor, December 7th and our beautiful bubble burst.

Up until then, we were just a couple of kids in love, who thought things would remain the same. We had never talked seriously about marriage, even though I guess that's what we both thought would eventually happen. I didn't know when this might be, but life was so wonderful, we coped with the minor people-problems everybody faces and didn't worry about the future. Dick didn't press me about marriage and I didn't pressure him.

At the beginning of World War Two, there weren't many qualified pilots. Dick was one of very few. He had enlisted in the Army Air Corps prior to coming to Atlanta and was called to active duty in the spring of 1942. It was May 10th, his mother's birthday.

He drove from Atlanta with another pilot to Wright Patterson Field in Dayton, Ohio, where he was to form a Troop Carrier Command; acting as a C-47 flight instructor of pilots with less than two hundred hours flying experience. A part of his job was to teach them to pull gliders and drop parachute troops in the 82nd Airborne Division.

He came by my place for a few minutes to say good-bye. We kept it upbeat. No tears or carrying on. I waved good-bye to Dick and he yelled back, "Don't take up with any 'cheapskates' while I'm gone!" He never let me forget what I had called him when we first met. His big smile was the last thing I saw of him for a while.

I kept busy with my job as Chief Stewardess with Delta and looked forward to my forthcoming promotion to Assistant Superintendent of Passenger Service. I felt proud of receiving the title and responsibility of Chief Stewardess, when Laura Wizark left to get married, five months after I had started. I vied with the rest of the girls in the initial class. Delta had the option of looking outside the company, although I knew that was not its general policy. I had worked hard. I felt I deserved it. I never was backward about going forward and I guess the Delta people liked that.

My job as Chief Stewardess was a demanding one. I was responsible for training all the new Delta stewardesses. My classes were small; maybe five or six girls. That's all we needed at the time.

I trained them how to serve meals on the plane and this proved to be a challenge for some. Some of the girls got so excited, they spilled the food on themselves, or worse yet, on somebody else. One day, I introduced a brand new trainee, who looked like a beautiful, voluptuous Petty girl model to one of Delta's handsome, red-blooded male pilots.

I said, "Joe, (not real name) I want you to meet Julie. (not real name). She's going to take good care of you."

Joe turned around and when he saw this exquisite example of feminine pulchritude, his eyes almost left their sockets.

In his most seductive, masculine voice, he said, "Julie, you can take care of me anytime you're ready!"

In her soft, most feminine seductive voice, Julie asked, "May I serve you a cup of coffee?"

He flashed his best sexy smile. "You bet!"

If Joe knew what he was going to get, he might not have been so eager. Julie made her way through the plane with the coffee and just as she started to hand the cup to him, she was so nervous, she tripped and the scalding hot liquid landed square in his lap.

Joe's reaction was spontaneous.

There was quite a flap about this incident for a few days. From then on, I never saw anyone as cautious as Joe, when he was served coffee, no matter how cute the girl was.

We didn't have a lot of the services we now take for granted, like computerized information on the flight schedules of other airlines, so part of my job was to teach the girls how to check the schedules of airlines, which had flights to places Delta didn't cover. In this way, we were able to help our customers, who transferred to another airline, to coordinate their flight plans. It was rare that a person was guided to the wrong flight and when it happened, the girl responsible for the error felt as bad about it as the unfortunate traveler, who found himself twenty thousand feet in the air, headed in the wrong direction. (Well, almost as bad.) There were tears and recriminations to contend with and my responsibility was to see that it didn't happen again.

One of my most enjoyable responsibilities was teaching the trainees about grooming. From the beginning, Delta was a stickler about appearance. This included instruction on acceptable hairstyles and make-up. The girls got a kick out of going to Rich's for professional make-up jobs and hair-dos.

Some of the trainees needed a little coaching in walking. I told them to point their feet straight in front of them, Indian style, instead of 'waddle walking' with the toes pointed out like a duck or chicken. Of course, when the air currents were strong, any style of walking in a plane from one point to another in a reasonably upright position was acceptable.

I taught the novices how to talk with the passengers to make them feel comfortable, how to cope with men who got too fresh, and reminded them: in all probability, the greatest use of their nursing expertise would be in helping passengers, who became nauseated. "Always remember the burp cups!" I also gave pointers on how to cope with a passenger's fear of flying.

I felt responsible for the girls I trained. They were generally hard-working, conscientious young women, who were excited about a wonderful opportunity to travel to places they'd never been before and meet new, interesting people.

I ran into a real stinker only once.

Audrey (not her real name) was a beautiful young girl from an affluent southern family; a brainy graduate of a fine women's college, who thought being a stewardess would be a temporary fun thing in her life. It was just that. She liked to show off her academic background by using five-syllable words. She flaunted her social position with constant name-dropping of prominent people her family knew. And whereas, most of the money-strapped trainees bought one uniform for spring and summer and one for fall and winter each year, Audrey kept a closet with seven new uniforms for each season. And her civies wardrobe was spectacular. She was the kind of person, who relished compliments, but never offered them in return. As a result, she stopped getting them.

Audrey may not have gone over big with the other stewardesses, but the pilots and male passengers were impressed. She looked a lot like Rita Hayworth, a gorgeous full-bodied woman, with a dynamic smile. She thought her good looks would let her get away with anything she wanted to do and eventually, we locked horns.

She had completed her training program and was being assigned to different flights. She was getting along reasonably well, until one Sunday, she called me about two hours before flight time. Her voice was weak.

"Birdie, I'm ill. I simply can't make it."

She sounded so pitiful, I felt sorry for her. "Don't you worry, Audrey. I'll handle it. Take care of yourself and let me know if I can help."

Delta didn't keep an extra supply of stand-by stewardesses. This meant if one of my girls became sick, I had to fill in for her. It was my job and I had to manage the best I could. That afternoon, it was an inconvenience to get myself together for an overnight flight to Fort Worth, but I made it and tried to be understanding.

That was the beginning. She tried this trick two more times, until someone kindly told me that Audrey was pulling my leg. I discovered that Audrey had a very active social life and she didn't want her job to interfere with her Saturday night fun. After my third unplanned trip on Audrey's behalf, another friend told me he had seen her whooping it up at a party, just a few hours before she called me.

That did it! The next day, I helped Audrey understand that being an airline stewardess was not her calling.

The last time I had to fill in for Audrey, it ruined my plans for a date with Dick and that was unacceptable. It took every ounce of self-control to keep from blowing sky high.

I was proud of myself for the fairly calm way I handled the situation and Audrey got the message very quickly.

We never met again.

Chapter 25

DICK'S PROPOSAL

From Dayton, Dick went to Kellogg Air Field, in Battle Creek, Michigan, where he continued his assignment as a C-47 flight instructor. Cross-country flights were a required part of the course and, somehow, Dick's flights always ended up in Atlanta. I never knew how he was able to do this, but the young men were thrilled to have an overnight stay in Atlanta, where they hoped to meet some pretty southern girls, even though they had to pay their own overnight expenses. Dick arranged their overnight passes. They stayed at the Hangar Hotel and most of the time, they went their way, while Dick and I went ours. Sometimes, we partied together and that was fun, too.

Every time, Dick and I saw each other, it got harder and harder for us to say goodbye and by the middle of July, Dick had had all he wanted of this arrangement. We had talked and joked about marriage, but nothing was ever definite, so it was a happy surprise when I received a letter from him which settled the matter.

Dick didn't write and ask me to marry him. He just said more or less, "Let's do it." The letter opened with the standard affectionate greeting and continued with the brief message that changed my life. It read: "Let's get married this next Saturday night when I come there. You can make all the arrangements. Just be sure Ham and Libby get the message so they can be married along with us." This blew me away! I was so excited the whole thing didn't quite register. I never dreamed I would take part in a double wedding! But, with prayerful thought, which lasted about a minute, I accepted the idea. I got on the phone with Libby, whom I hadn't seen for a while. Ham Todd was an Eastern captain and I guess he and Dick must have talked about this earlier. It was the first time I knew anything about it, but I was so happy, I didn't care. If Ham and Libby wanted to make it a double wedding, it was all right with me.

Libby was thrilled with the idea, and from then on, it was a madhouse. There was so much to be done and so little time to do it. I scarcely knew where to turn first. Libby went along with me on the idea of having the wedding at the College Park

Methodist Church, where a distant cousin of mine, John Tate, was the pastor.

Several weeks earlier, Dick had helped me solve the problem of what my wedding outfit would be. He had come home on an overnight pass with his students and while here, we went out to dinner and I noticed some clothes in the backseat of the car.

I asked, "What are you going to do with those clothes, Dick?"

"They're going to the Salvation Army. I can't wear them until after the war is over. No telling how long that'll be. Somebody else might as well get some good out of them."

I teased, "That's a beautiful white suit back there. It looks like new. I could make a wedding suit out of it. I want it!"

He didn't take me up on my blatant suggestion. He didn't say one word about getting married. He just turned and smiled. "It's yours, Birdie."

So Dick's used suit became my wedding outfit. The day Dick's letter arrived, I took the suit to a seamstress in Hapeville, near the airport. We talked about how it would be designed and she had it ready the day before the wedding. I know she must have worked awfully hard, because making a suit in just a few days is no small task. I can't remember her name, but I've never forgotten how kind that lady was to me.

The state of my personal economy was at an all-time low. I didn't have an extra dime to spend on a trousseau, so everything else I had was either already in my wardrobe, or borrowed. To follow the old saying about having something old, something new, something borrowed, and something blue to bring good luck, I wore a borrowed blue garter. That fulfilled two requirements. My lovely white suit was new to me, so I considered it as such. And my big white hat with a bow on it was old; something I'd had at least a couple of years.

I knew Delta's policy about stewardesses having to leave when they got married. I should. I'd been preaching it to my trainees for nearly two years. I loved flying and although I was happy and smiling, there was a lump in my throat, when I announced I was getting married in a few days.

Mr. Cushing made it hard on me. He said, "Birdie, you're here. You're trained. Just stay."

My lower lip started quivering. "Mr. Cushing, you know I can't do that. It's against the rules."

He barked, "Let me worry about the rules! I don't want you to go! I want you to stay!"

The tears started rolling down my face. I felt so strongly that a bride should be with her husband.

Cushing wouldn't let up. "I have a daughter who's married and she's staying here in Atlanta. And Dick comes down to see you every weekend. You don't have anything to worry about. You should stay!"

He made me feel rotten, like I was doing something terribly disloyal to leave the airline, when I was needed, so I threw out a suggestion. "Mr. Cushing, would you ask Dick if he'll let me stay."

Mr. Cushing exploded. "No! Dammit! I'm not marrying him. You are! You ask him!"

Things got tense. I sat there and said nothing. And Mr. Cushing sat there stewing for a minute, til he realized it was a lost cause.

I rose to go and he came around the side of his desk, put his arm around me and tried to smooth things over. "Well, Birdie, you might as well get married and go with him, because you're wasting the government's money with Dick dashing down here every weekend in an Army Air Force plane to see you."

That was not accurate. Dick did come to see me when he could arrange it, but it was not every weekend and when he came, he combined his trip with his responsibility to instruct his students on cross country flight. I will admit things were different the day we were married. What happened did exceed normal procedure. Dick's explanation: "It was a lack of communication."

On our wedding day, Dick scheduled a cross country flight for his students. The main problem was the scarcity of gasoline and the fact that he was issued only enough to get to Nashville, Tennessee. I'm sure Dick had this thing worked out in his head in advance, because Atlanta was where he had to go in order to get married and Nashville is about two hundred miles shy of the target.

As long as I knew him, Dick always had friends all over everywhere and it turned out that he had a friend at the airfield in Nashville. When he got there, he ran into Al Gasser's office (no pun intended, that was his real name). Dick told him, "You have to get me some gas. I'm getting married tonight in Atlanta and I've got to get there!"

Al Gasser took pity on Dick. "Well, son of a gun! We'll give you a little gas and see if we can't help you get squared away with your headquarters." He added, "Go ahead and send a

R.O.N. (request to remain overnight) and fill 'erup!"

It was raining when Dick landed in Nashville and was still raining when he and his students piled back into the plane. Everything was going great til he ran into an electrical storm and the students got excited about a couple of surprise drops in altitude.

One yelled, "God amighty! This is better than a roller-coaster!"

Things eased up a bit til they approached Atlanta, when the weather started doing all sorts of wild things, with thunder booming and lightning flashing across the sky, like fireworks on the fourth of July. The radio went bad and when a message came through, Dick said he couldn't be sure what it was. He said the voice sounded kind of excited.

It was.

The man at the control tower was screaming, "Don't land!" Dick said he couldn't make it out.

He landed. Dick said it was a rough landing. His students said it was masterful. And with hoots and howls of praise from his trainees, he deplaned and was told to report to the commanding officer 'on the double'.

Dick suspected trouble. But again, he knew the commanding officer and hoped that might help. It did. He walked into Colonel Outlaw's office. The colonel had his eyes fixed on some papers on his desk. He showed signs of agitation. He continued to look at his report, then yelled, "Lieutenant, you had clear orders not to land!"

"Colonel Outlaw, the orders may have been clear at this end, but with the storm, the radio reception in the plane was lousy." Colonel Outlaw looked up and recognized Dick.

"You old son of a gun! What're you doing here?"

"First, I'm getting chewed out. Second, I'm getting married in a few hours and I don't even have a license!"

The colonel warmed up, but admonished, "Dick, what you did was very dangerous. Next time, be sure about your landing orders." Then he smiled, rose from his desk and put his hand on Dick's shoulder as he pushed him out the door. "Go on! Don't worry about it now. And best wishes to you and your bride!"

When Dick left the colonel's office, I greeted him, along with his five students. They were waiting to find out what had happened and we were all relieved to know that the colonel was a man of understanding. Dick told his energetic students, "You're on your own for a few hours."

I chirped, "Y'all have a ball! And bring a girl friend to the wedding!"

Dick reminded them. "Don't forget. You guys are going with us on our honeymoon in the morning. Time of departure is 10 A.M. We'll meet you in the lobby."

Dick and I walked into the courthouse hand in hand. A friendly clerk took one look and asked, "Would you like to go ahead and have the ceremony here?"

I extended an invitation. "We're having a double wedding this evening at the College Park Methodist Church and you're invited."

She smiled and said she had other plans. She was nice about it, but I felt her reaction didn't do justice to the occasion. After all, Dick and I and Ham and Libby were getting married and that made it about the most important event of the decade.

Chapter 26
THE DOUBLE WEDDING

Saturday, July 25, 1942. Early in the morning, I spread the word around to my fellow workers that I was getting married that evening. I put an announcement on the bulletin board at Delta. Ham and Libby put one at Eastern. Mine was short and sweet: "I'm getting married tonight to Dick Bomar at 8 P.M. at the College Park Methodist Church. It's a double wedding! Y'all come! Get two for the price of one! Birdie Perkins."

There was no time or money for engraved invitations and the bulletin board was a great way to get the word around. The airline workers were like a big family. We were interested in what happened to each other and everybody I talked to seemed excited about the double wedding. I can't guarantee what happened at Eastern. At Delta, as news of the blanket invitation got around, folks started making plans to attend and in anticipation of the happy event, the celebrating began. A bunch of mechanics and pilots who got the news as they completed their shift, started partying early in the day. And later, I heard that a few stout souls partied more than they should have.

One was a tall guy name Charlie. As a result, he got so carried away with emotion, he showed up in church with a shotgun and announced, "I'm gonna see that this thing goes the way it should!"

My cousin, who was performing the ceremony, brought his wife and left her to mingle with the crowd, while he went to get ready. Cousin Nettie observed Charlie's performance with interest. She could hardly have missed it. She went to assist him.

She was a wee bit of a thing, but she had had a lot of experience being a preacher's wife and she had mastered the art of coping in difficult situations with difficult people. Seeing that Charlie's conduct was exceeding the bounds of good taste, calmly and quietly, she went to him, gently lifted the shotgun from his hands, looked up and told him.

"We can't act like that. This is the house of the Lord."

She turned to a good friend of mine and asked her to take care of Charlie, while Nettie took the gun to her husband's office. Katherine sat Charlie down beside her, held his hand and tried to calm him. She soon found that gentleness worked only so far.

While the church was filling up with jubilant, enthusiastic guests, my friend, Peg White, sang a couple of songs. She had a sweet clear voice and I was pleased that she agreed to share her talent at our wedding. Peg had to do a great deal of soul searching before she agreed to perform. The dilemma: Peg was a catholic and she didn't think she ought to perform in a protestant church. A further dilemma: she really wanted to sing. The solution: she finally decided if she sang from the balcony, it was far enough away from the scene of action that surely the Lord would forgive her. So, to ease her conscience, that's where she performed. She sang "Because" and when she began "I Love You Truly", Charlie lost control. In a voice so loud, even Dick heard it, he said, "Let's harmonize!"

Katherine was brief. She said, "Shut up!" Those were the last words Dick heard until the pianist started the first chords of "Here Comes the Bride".

Those of us getting married were sorry more members of our family weren't able to be with us, but everything had been put together so quickly, they couldn't make it. Ham and Dick acted as each other's best man; Ham in his civies and Dick in his uniform. Libby and I were both lucky enough to have our sisters with us as bridesmaids. All the girls wore street length dresses.

I was a few minutes late. A run in my stocking. I ran over to Libby. Everybody was waiting on me. The procession was ready to start and I was so nervous, I scarcely knew what was happening. Lema turned around, looked at me and announced the happy news, 'Birdie, your hat's about to fall off." Every bride wants to look her best and Lema's information was not comforting. Libby calmly straightened my chapeau.

It had started to rain, but inside, the church was over-flowing with excited friends and a few relatives. Seating space had disappeared early. Folks were standing against the walls, in the back of the church, and in a packed balcony. It was not a sedate gathering. Happy chattering and laughter filled the air. Dick's proud students had a place of honor on the front row, with shining faces and a pretty girl by each one of them. There had been too much advance celebration for many of the folks to sit quietly, but fortunately, most of them were not as noisy as Charlie.

With the opening chords of the wedding march, the gathering became quiet. Lema and Libby's sister walked down the aisle separately; then Libby and I walked down together. Libby was a tall beautiful blond and I know she wore a white outfit of some description. I know I wore Dick's made-over white suit with a big white hat. I remember some of the preacher's words, like "Do you take this man?" and "Do you take this woman?" and the four yesses and "I now pronounce you man and wife." I remember getting a ring and a quick kiss and all the rest is a happy blur, with cameras flashing. Somebody had called the local newspaper about our double wedding and it was covered by the Associated Press. I still don't remember promising to obey and have mentioned this to Dick on more than one occasion.

After the ceremony, everybody went to a big whoop-t-doo party at the Hangar Hotel, put on by the hostess of the dining room, courtesy of the hotel, which thought it was good public relations, since all of us who got married were associated with the airlines. The management of the hotel was pleased that the Associated Press got wind of the double wedding and the fact that it was written up and sent to newspapers and radio stations throughout the United States.

Dick and I had met in the rain and got married in the rain. We had met at the Hangar Hotel and spent our wedding night there.

I think we were both somewhat in shock, since everything had happened so fast, but we were elated and in love and for a brief time, we closed the door against all the gaiety and laughter of the present, the uncertainty of the future, and drifted off in our own private world, wrapped in the security of each other's arms.

* * * * * * * * *

Dick and I had never discussed the possibility of going on a honeymoon. With his military commitment, we knew it was out of the question. I didn't worry about it. I just knew I was going to be with him.

A few days before the wedding, he had called on the phone and told me he was going to take me back to Kellogg Air Field the day after the wedding.

I asked, "How?"

"You'll have to ride with me and my students."

"Dick, is it standard procedure for a bride to ride with her new husband in an Air Force plane?"

Rules and regulations had to be followed and I was worried.

Dick changed the subject abruptly. That's when I knew something had to be done. And I did it.

Sometimes, when I look back on the times when I've acted in haste without giving due consideration to the consequences, I don't know how I ever did those things. This was one of those times. My one track mind was set firmly on getting permission to ride back with Dick in the Air Force plane after the wedding and this thought propelled me into the office of the major at the Atlanta Air Base. I had been doing some public relations work for the major at his request. When I approached him, he probably thought he had made a poor choice and my brazen manner could have played havoc with a pleasant relationship.

Without the benefit of any advance social amenity, I blurted out, "Major, I'm going to get married this Saturday night. And I'm going to fly away in an Army airplane with my husband, and I don't want to hear a word about it out of you, or anybody else!"

The major was momentarily quiet, but his surprise at my outburst was apparent. It was a tense moment. I didn't know whether he was going to blow up, or not.

He didn't. I guess those in charge sometimes tried to help young people during the war.

He said quietly, "Okay, Miss Perkins. Go ahead. You won't hear a word out of me. Go ahead and do what you've planned to do. At this point, I imagine you're going to do it anyway." He was so nice about it, I felt guilty that I had been so cocky. The remorse didn't last long.

After the wedding and the first party of the evening at the Hangar Hotel, we moved to the home of a friend on West Mercer, where people partied most of the night. It was here that our friend, Buddy the Bat Man, approached Dick and me.

"When you two love birds get packed and ready to go in the morning, I'll drive you out to the plane."

True to his word, the next morning, Buddy drove up in his big, yellow Buick convertible, with the top down. The sun was shining and a soft breeze cooled the summer heat. Dick had to leave early to check on the plane and his students, but Lema and my other roommate, Kathryn, were there. Buddy took charge, "Okay, Birdie, I want you and your sister to sit up on the back of the seat. He flirted with Kathryn and told her, "You may have the pleasure of sitting by me."

We all piled in and away we went to the airfield, waving and shouting to well wishers along the way. Buddy was so delighted with himself and his mission, he drove right up to the plane, which was strictly against regulations. Dick met us there with his five smiling students. I said good-bye to Lema, who had to shed a tear or two. Then I marched over and boarded the aircraft beside Dick, in front of anybody who happened to be looking. Why we didn't get into a barrel of trouble, I'll never know. They say all the world loves a lover. The major must have decided to look the other way, while Dick and I and the five students took off for Battle Creek on our honeymoon.

The flight progressed smoothly til we made a stop in Chicago, where we took time out to eat an ice cream cone. As a new bride, I was having a ball, even though I was the only girl among all those men; or maybe I was enjoying it because I was the only female.

Dick was in a benevolent mood, after having just gotten married, and proud of himself for having arranged the transportation so well. Just as if I hadn't had anything to do with it. So he decided to let a very nervous young student takeoff. My intuition told me this was a mistake. The young man was so unstrung, when we first became airborne, he veered the plane sharply. I was sure we were headed for a crack-up and I was such a new bride, I wasn't ready to die.

I screamed at Dick, "Take the controls quick! He's going to crash!" The young man was perspiring. I was perspiring. The rest of the students looked pale. And Dick was cool as a cucumber.

His voice was as calm as could be. "Birdie, take it easy. I have everything under control."

Looking from a forty-five degree angle, fifty feet above the ground, I wasn't too sure. The students looked like they didn't feel to sure, either. A couple of them were white as a lily.

The rest of the trip was uneventful. Thank you, Lord.

I still think Dick is the most wonderful man I've ever known, but I'll have to admit, he had a strange habit of pulling surprises on me. What came next was one of my early exposures to this trait.

It must have been all the quiet around him, because after our exhilarating take-off, nobody had much to say. I guess we were all just glad to be alive.

During the lull, Dick started taking a guilt trip about everything that had happened in the last twenty-four hours: mainly his conniving personal use of government property. He didn't share his thoughts. He simply made a decision to confess what he'd done and, of course, this in turn, changed what happened next.

The original plan was to land in Kalamazoo, where Charlie Lewelle, an American Airlines pilot from Memphis, was to pick me up at the airport and take me to Kellogg Field in Battle Creek. Dick and his students were also to fly to Kellogg, where we would "meet," since I was not supposed to have been flying in the Air Force plane. This arrangement didn't turn me on, but for once I hadn't opened my mouth and I was glad, because Dick's conscience started gnawing on him overtime.

As we approached Kalamazoo, Dick announced, 'I'm not going to do this! I'm taking you to Battle Creek with me!" I was delighted.

When we deplaned and parted from our little friends, Dick asked me to wait for him and he strode into Captain Minnick's office and made his soul-searched confession.

"I've done a terrible thing." Then he laid his cards on the table. "Captain Minnick, I've taken an Air Force plane and gone with my students, not just to Nashville, as originally scheduled, but on to Atlanta to get married. What's more, I have just landed with my five students and my brand new bride, who had no right to be in that plane."

While the captain looked on in amazement and admiration, Dick continued. "I had planned to compound the deception by leaving her in Kalamazoo, but I couldn't do it!"

Captain Minnick didn't bat an eye over this heart-wrenching confession. He broke out in a lusty guffaw and agreed loudly, "That's a dammed good idea! My family is way out in Wisconsin and this next weekend, I'm going to go there and get my wife, and my kids and my dogs and bring 'em all back here! "He stood. Slammed his left hand flat on his desk and extended his right one to Dick. "It's not good for married folks to be separated!"

Charlie vacated the apartment he and Dick shared, to let us have some privacy, and we honeymooned in Battle Creek for about a month.

Chapter 27

OVERSEAS WITH A MADE-TO-ORDER BED

During the period when Dick trained the young pilots here in the states, he got a big thrill towing the first CG-4A glider from the East Coast to California. Dick loved his work.

He loved teaching the men to fly and realized that their future safety depended on his thoroughness and attention to detail. I was happy for him, even though there were many times I felt at loose ends, since I'd been used to working outside the home nearly all my life.

Dick's working hours could be any time of the day or night. I can remember many times when I went to meet him and curled up in the car and slept until three in the morning, waiting for him to finish instructing his students in night flight.

I knew the time was fast approaching when Dick would be transferred overseas and I dreaded the thought. I tried not to let Dick know how concerned I was and tried to convince myself the Lord would look after him, when I couldn't be around to do it. If I had thought I could get by with it, I would have stowed away in his plane and gone with him into battle.

The grim news finally came. Dick was scheduled to go overseas May 10, 1943. His call to service came again on his mother's birthday. He left from Fort Benning, Columbus, Georgia, where we shared a private home with another couple.

We had had ten wonderful, unforgettable months since our wedding; months that were crowded to the fullest with all the love, excitement and drama that can only be experienced during war, when you're constantly living on the edge of uncertainty, filled with mixed emotions that are hard to put into words.

During Dick's off-hours, we relaxed and laughed with our many new acquaintances at the base. We heard all the scary reports from Europe and never doubted there would be anything other than final victory for 'our side.'

I was still a relatively new bride and I felt like my heart was going to be wrenched out of me at the thought of Dick going away. And I worried. I worried about the great danger which would face him everyday. This one I turned over to God, because I knew I had no control in that area and promised to pray daily. I also worried about lesser matters. I worried about him not getting the right kind of food, and aside from the things I planned to send him, I knew this, too, would be out of my hands and reluctantly turned that matter over to God. Then I started worrying about the places he'd be sleeping. With a vivid imagination, I could see him trying to sleep on the hard ground, with every kind of danger lurking around. I was particularly caught up with the idea that he might be attacked by tarantulas and I said, "Lord, I think I can take care of this one."

I decided Dick should have a bed to take with him; his very own private bed. And with this driving goal in mind, I looked in the phone directory and to my delight, I found a mattress factory in Columbus. I marched into the mattress factory on May 9th and demanded to see the manager. A pleasant looking man appeared and asked, "How may I help you?"

I started a little awkwardly. "Sir, I've been out all morning collecting tooth paste and toilet paper."

"Madam, I'm sorry. We don't carry those items."

"Sir, what I'm trying to tell you is that my husband is going overseas."

"Madam, I'm sorry to hear that, but I don't think I can be of any help."

"Oh, yes you can."

"How's that?"

"I want to have a bed made for him."

The nice man brightened. "Well, I think we can handle that. What did you have in mind?"

I held my hand about a foot above the counter. "I want a mattress; a foot to a foot and a half deep."

"I'm sure we can make the mattress for you, but we're under a lot of pressure right now."

I started getting frantic. "Mister, I've got to have this mattress right away! My husband is going on maneuvers and I'm worried about tarantulas. And I want him to have a bed so he won't have to sleep on the ground in his tent!"

The manager saw how desperate and determined I was. He chuckled. "Don't panic. I'll get it done for you." He started writing up the order. "Fill in this form. That'll be ten dollars up front."

I gave him a ten spot and he asked, "How do you plan to get this bed overseas?"

"I'm going to put it on his plane. He's a pilot, so he'll be flying his own plane over."

He seemed amused at my explanation. "I see you have it all worked out. Now, when do you want the bed?"

"He's leaving tomorrow evening at six."

The nice manager paled and lost his smile completely, but promised to have it ready.

That evening, I told Dick about the mattress-bed. "I've had that bed made especially for you, because I'm worried about you sleeping on the ground. I'm worried about tarantulas getting you." This must have been a comforting thought for him. I continued: "I want you to promise that you'll take it with you and use it as long as you're overseas," and added a word of admonition: "I don't want you sharing it with tarantulas, or anybody else!"

The mattress factory manager had a beautiful bed made for Dick and had it delivered out to Fort Benning and put on his plane. He was a good man.

Goodbye time was hard. Dick was pleased with the bed he was taking into combat. He laughed and tried to make light of the parting, promising me that he wouldn't share his bed with anyone else til he came home and we shared it together. And I started bossing him around and telling him to be careful and try to eat right and to always keep his eyes open for the enemy and not to go around in wet clothes and just about anything else I could think of, with the final command: "Now, you be sure to write!"

The word had gotten around about Dick's bed and when his crew was boarding the plane, there was a lot of laughing and kidding Dick, and in the midst of all this lightheartedness, while other loved ones were waving back and forth, the door to the plane closed and I stood there and watched my heart taxi down the runway. There was a large crowd on hand. Mothers and fathers, girl friends, wives, children, and a few babes in arms. Some of the people were laughing, trying to keep the parting upbeat. Many of the women were crying. I was one of them. I found the tears running down my face as I watched his plane in formation grow smaller and smaller, til it was finally just a little dot in the sky. And then it was gone.

Life without Dick was terribly empty, but there was consolation in knowing I was not alone. Many of the women I knew were without their husbands. There was a strong feeling of patriotism and most of them who had no children, or those who were able to make provisions for child care, busied themselves in war related jobs. But, when Dick went to war, I went back to Delta.

This was unheard of earlier. There had always been a hard and fast rule that once you got married, you lost your job. None of the airlines I knew of allowed married women to work for them. This changed. Actually, things began to change when the Japanese bombed Pearl Harbor. Right after that, Mr. Woolman called me into his office and told me, "As of now, we are dropping our requirement for our stewardesses to be registered nurses. We are going to encourage our present stewardesses to join the service to help with the war effort. I'm sure this is going to create a personnel problem but I don't think it'll be too hard on you. From now on, we'll accept any young women who meet our other requirements."

The airlines still wouldn't hire any woman, who was too short, too fat, too old, or pregnant. But, the departure from hiring only registered nurses was a radical change. The departure from hiring married women was another. I was Delta's first married stewardess.

Lifting the ban on those who were married and those who weren't nurses was welcomed news. It created a fine opportunity for women who were looking for jobs while their husbands were in the service. It was a boon for others, who didn't want to go through the lengthy, strenuous training to become a registered nurse.

Air travel had progressed to the point where registered nurses were not thought to be as necessary to the welfare of the passengers as they had been in the past. And married women were found to be more dependable than previously imagined.

Chapter 28
THE INVASION OF SICILY

Dick's tour of duty overseas was brief. When he'd been gone two months, he was wounded. But during the time he was there, his then-famous mattress-bed went everywhere he went. In North Africa, its fame spread. It became a source of envy among the servicemen and a former TWA pilot, George Faulkner, who shared a tent with Dick and had surreptitiously nap-tested its comfort, was so impressed, he wrote and repeated an earlier request, "If anything happens to Dick, may I have his bed?"

This was after Dick was wounded and although his life wasn't threatened, I thought the TWA pilot was short on tact and told him so. He was unrepentant.

There was a lot of coveting going on about Dick's bed, while he was using it. He handled the situation as tactfully as possible and told me later he didn't know what he would have done without it. I guess he'd have done what all the rest of the men did and do without. But I'm glad he had it to make life a little easier during that period.

Dick was stationed in Tangiers. I was confident it was a prime breeding area for tarantulas. And I prayed the mattress-bed would provide some protection.

He went over as a captain and was promoted to major. His initial responsibility was serving as Flight Operations Officer in the 62nd Troop Carrier Squadron. He then rose to Squadron Commander of the 32nd Squadron. He was one of the first to fly over the beachhead to drop paratroopers during the invasion of Sicily.

Dick flew his first mission of the invasion and hit his drop zone with the paratroopers. The second night, he didn't go because winds were too strong over the Mediterranean to allow a successful flight. The third night, July 11, 1943, fate intervened to bring Dick home from the war. I just wish he could have come back in better condition.

Dick had not planned to go on this third mission. At the last minute, he and three other squadron commanders decided to give some of the students they'd trained the opportunity to get credit for this mission. Dick's co-pilot was David Rosencrants (now retired Lieutenant Colonel U.S.A.F.) a young man everybody called Rosie. Dick let Rosie take the controls. He had had a good flight and it was an important one. This was the beginning of the invasion of Sicily and its success depended on this mission.

Dick's goal was to hit a drop zone where a fire was to be lit as a signal and reference point for the batteries of our war ships out in the Mediterranean. They had reached their target. The paratroops were dropped. The fires were lit. The mission was a success. They had just turned around, when Dick said, "Rosie, you've done a good job! Now I'll take her home." They swapped seats and five minutes later, all hell broke loose.

The war ships started shelling. The enemy began an intense counter attack and Dick's aircraft was caught in the cross-fire, flying at 500 feet with the windows open. They were caught in a barrage of bullets. A shell exploded in the cockpit, blowing a gaping hole in the ceiling. Dick felt his wrist burn and when the smoke and dust settled, Rosie asked Dick if he was hurt.

Dick held up his arm. His left hand dangled loosely by a small strip of skin. "Yes, damn it! Thirteen years of flying and a career shot to hell!"

His wrist was shattered. He was shot in the leg. Blood covered the cockpit, the men, the seats, the controls, the windshield. Some of their control cables had been shot away and Dick was sure they were going to crash in the ocean.

He went wild. He yelled, "Give me a knife! I'm going to cut this thing off! I can't swim like this!"

Rosie yelled back. "NO! You are not going to lose your hand and we're not going to crash! The Flight Surgeon has taught us how to deal with these injuries! We're not going to cut it off!"

Dick had taught his men how to fly the plane with the controls locked by using the engines. One of the flight crew gave Dick first aid, a shot of morphine and sulfa drugs and Rosie said emphatically, "We're going to get back safe! And we're going to save your hand!"

Rosie was the hero of the hour, even if he did almost demolish a jeep on the runway. The poor guy had to land a crippled plane with no flaps and almost no control.

Captain Broun, the squadron doctor, went with Dick to the hospital. He examined the wound and told him, "I'm sorry. I see no way of saving your hand. There's nothing to do but amputate."

It was a soul-wrenching experience for the man I love, who was always in control of every situation. He broke down and cried. He pleaded with the doctor not to cut off his hand.

"Please! Captain, don't do it! The only thing I know how to do is fly and if you take my hand, I'll never be able to fly again!"

Captain Broun left the room for a few minutes. When he returned, he still looked dead serious.

"All right, Major Bomar. There's one thing we can do. We can give you three days. If your hand starts to turn blue, it'll have to come off immediately. And it'll have to come off even higher up your arm. We'll give you that much of a chance."

Three days later, the doctor examined Dick's hand. It had started turning pink!

The doctor had attached his hand with hooks and bolts and the long healing process began. The wound in his left leg gave him a lot of trouble, but it was nothing in comparison with the intense pain in his hand. Dick remained in hospitals overseas from July 11th, the day of his injury, until September, when he was returned to the United States.

Shortly after Dick went through the painful procedure of having his hand attached with the mechanical devices, he was transferred by train to Algiers. The long, rough ride caused considerable trauma. The bolts were jolted out of place and he had to go through the painful process of being rebolted.

I know there were many young men who fought in the war and paid a much higher price than Dick, but his injury took a serious toll on him. When he returned to New York, he had gone from 160 to 130 pounds. He was skin and bones.

When I received word that Dick was coming back to the States, I was overjoyed. I immediately turned in my second resignation to Delta and headed for New York.

During that period of the war, all seats were classified as "priority". They were reserved for VIPs, state department officials and servicemen. I didn't come under any of these categories, but I was lucky. My sister, Lema, worked for Eastern. She heard about a last minute cancellation. I heard about it a few minutes later and everything was under control.

My excitement grew by leaps and bounds. I was going to see Dick again. I was going to visit New York for the first time. With all the traveling I had done, I had never been to this fabulous city and I boldly flew into unknown territory, with no plans and no knowledge about where I should spend the night before going to Staten Island early the next day.

The plane arrived in New York at midnight. The captain tried to be nice to me. He said, "Birdie, you've never been in New York City before. You don't know your way around and it's not good for you to be out on the streets by yourself. You ought to come with me. My wife will be happy to have you stay overnight."

I had on one of those crazy hats which were popular at the time. It had a long feather in it and everytime I turned to talk to anybody, I had to be careful about my aim. As I tried to manage my tote bag and be pleasant to the captain, who was trying so hard to be cordial and protective, I almost got him in the eye.

"Thanks so much, but no thanks. I have to go to Staten Island first thing in the morning out to Holleran General Hospital. I'd rather go to a hotel for a few hours, because I plan to leave at daybreak."

"Birdie, you shouldn't be out on the streets alone!"

"Thanks. I'll manage." I was just as hardheaded as usual, when I've made up my mind about something. And after several narrow escapes of lancing him with my feather, I deplaned and struck out on my own.

I thought I knew what I was doing. I was confident and brave (foolhardy would be a better word) about what lay ahead. My first goal was to get to the area of the ferry where I would board next morning. A porter at the airport gave me instructions how to get on the right subway, which would go to the ferry.

While waiting for the subway, I ran into some servicemen and grabbed one by the arm. "Hey! I have to get to Staten Island. I need you to help me!"

The nice young private with a big grin and G.I. crew cut said, "Sure, lady!"

The train stopped in front of us. He picked up my bags and helped me on the train, as I tried to aim my feather in the other direction. I found out that one of the young men in the group was a ward boy at Holleran General. He told me, "It's fun riding on the ferry. It costs a nickel."

I was so nervous, I fumbled around with my purse and couldn't get to my coins. My distress was obvious. The nice ward boy flashed a smile and quickly planted a nickel in the palm of my hand. He said, "Be my guest!"

He got off at the ferry station with me and asked, "What are you going to do now?"

"I'm going to find a room where I can sleep for a few hours."

Just before he left, he said, "Mam, you shouldn't be out on the streets alone in this neighborhood at night."

"I'll be fine. You just go up there and find Major Bomar tonight and tell him I'm here in New York and I'll be there as soon as I can in the morning."

I knew he'd wake Dick up in the middle of the night, but I wanted him to know I was coming. The young man was so nice about wanting to help.

We parted and I started in search of a hotel close to the ferry. Outside the subway station, I looked in all directions and about a block away I saw a lighted sign, which looked like it might be a hotel. The closer I came, the less desirable it looked, but I was dead tired and almost broke and it looked like it might be cheap. It was.

I entered the dimly-lighted, seedy-looking lobby, went to the registration desk and addressed the clerk. "Could I get a room for just a few hours?"

The disheveled man with several days growth of beard smiled at me in a knowing way. "Miss, we'll be glad to let you have a room for just an hour. That's the most popular time, but if you need it for longer, that's okay, too."

That's when it hit me. I realized that my surroundings were somewhat less than pristine. I thought, "Good grief! It's a flophouse!"

I was so tired, I was desperate for a place to rest for awhile. I pretended I didn't know what the clerk was talking about and told him, "I have to catch the ferry first thing in the morning. I'm going to see my wounded husband who's just come home from the war on a hospital ship."

He spat in an old dented brass spittoon and listened in a disinterested way. "My husband was on the Seminole, which used to be an excursion ship. On the way over, they ran into the worst storm the captain said he'd ever seen."

The clerk broke in. "Mam, it's hitting right at three. We'll rent it to you til six. That'll be a dollar fifty."

Rebuffed and weary, I turned to go to my room. On the way, I saw two couples in the hallway. Both women were dressed in cheap, fancy outfits I wouldn't be caught dead in. They were both satin. One wore bright red with thin rhinestone straps and no back. The other sported black, with a bunch of tacky feathers around the hem. The red hot mama was a platinum blond with frizzy hair that looked like it hadn't had a shampoo in a month. The lady of the night in black had the most interesting shade of red hair I'd ever seen. It made mine look pale in comparison.

Their escorts were greasy-looking slime-balls, with slicked-back, black hair, zoot suits and wide-brim slouch hats that made them look like a couple of two-bit gangsters. It was obvious all four were high on something. They were laughing and talking as loud as could be, with no regard for anybody trying to sleep. Then the thought occurred: not many folks used these accommodations for sleeping.

My room qualified for immediate attention by the city health department. It stank of stale smoke and alcohol and in the midst of dog days, it was hot as blazes. A miserable little fan in the window did its best, but it was a losing battle.

The clerk's comments gave fair warning about noise and just as I stretched out, it began. For two hours, a man and woman in the room next to mine indulged in a remarkable amount of exercise. I could hear the bed thumping around, while the mattress springs squeaked, and above it all, giggles, groans and occasional "My Gods!" til I felt the blood rush to my face, despite the fact that nobody could see me blushing. For a young married woman, who had been protected all her life and brought up with high moral standards, this unsolicited education regarding the sexual practices of some people was flabbergasting, non-redeeming and certainly unwanted. In the midst of the entertainment, I felt something bite me. I turned on the light, threw back the sheet and saw three or four fleas jumping around in happy anticipation of a feast. I captured the little beasts, flushed them down the john, and after a couple of repeat performances with a new cast of creatures, things quieted down and I got an hour's sleep.

The morning desk clerk was sensitive enough to realize I was in the wrong surroundings. The night clerk must have told him I didn't know which end was up; a dumb little southern girl, who'd never been to New York before, and I guess he felt sorry for me. The morning guy was sympathetic when I told him how I was up there to be with my wounded husband.

I told him, "I didn't get but one hour's sleep. You ought to give me back a dollar!"

"Sorry, mam. I can't do that." He tried to be nice, but I'm sure he wanted me to go as quickly as possible.

As I was leaving, I told him. "This place has fleas!"

He said, "Yes, mam."

It was a shocking experience. And it was a long times before I could bring myself to tell Dick. I knew he would have hit the ceiling and in his condition, I didn't want him to get upset. He had enough problems.

After I checked out of the hotel, I got a bite to eat at a small cafe down the street.

The ferry ride was pleasant. I watched the early morning sun glisten on the water, looked at the sleepy faces of the passengers, and thought about Dick, as I listened to the water gently splash against the side of the boat. It was a welcome time of quiet before we docked and I hailed a cab.

Holleran General was mammoth. It must have been ten times the size of South Highland, but I felt sure I could find my way around. People generally think of hospitals as being very much alike. They're wrong. Hospital have personalities just like people do. Some are nice and friendly. Some are cold and indifferent. Holleran General was a military hospital. Strong on attention to the patients, but not so interested in strangers. I thought they needed a little instruction in southern hospitality.

The ward boy I met the night before had told Dick I was on the island and he was waiting for me.

My first glimpse of him was at the end of a long hall. I could see him sitting by a window in a small public area, talking to a man next to him. They were both in wheel chairs. He looked so pale and thin.

When he saw me, a faint smile appeared and I heard him say, "There's Birdie, feather and all." I had on my glamorous hat with the long feather to cheer him up. Obviously, it was needed.

The reunion was emotional. It was also smelly.

As I approached him, I got a good whiff. And the closer I came, the worse it got. He smelled awful! You could have smelled him a block away! I knew it was from the drainage in his arm.

I also knew the drainage meant it had a good chance of healing.

Chapter 29
THE TRANSFER

Through the kindness of one of the workers at the hospital, Dick and I had a three-day honeymoon of sorts. You couldn't call it a second honeymoon, because we'd never had a real one to begin with.

A nice young nurse had heard about my coming up to get Dick and told us, "You can have my apartment for three days while I'm away. There's no reason why you shouldn't use it. Dick can walk, if he wants to. He doesn't have to be in that wheelchair." So, for three days, Dick and I had a little time to ourselves to get reacquainted and I had a chance to fuss over him and boss him around and make him do what he ought to do to get well. It was a nice little apartment two miles from the hospital, an easy commute by taxi.

Each day, we went to Holleran from nine to five, just as if Dick had a job. And he did. The job was for Dick to go through all kinds of testing and evaluations concerning the condition of his hand to see if the doctors could save it.

Dick's morale was low. He was still afraid he might lose his hand and a good part of his left arm and he knew if that were to happen, he wouldn't be able to continue flying and that was all he knew how to do; all he really wanted to do. When I think about Dick and his love of flying, it reminds me of the verse: "Blessed is he who has found his work." Dick had found his life's work in being a pilot. He really loved it. And, although, I knew that I would love him just the same, with or without his hand, I grieved for him and prayed he wouldn't lose it.

During those first three days, Dick started to perk up and I saw signs of his sense of humor returning. On the third day at lunchtime, Dick called playfully to a buddy he hadn't seen at the hospital before. "Come here. I want you to meet Seasick Sylvester."

His pal came over and he and Dick went through a brief ritual of smiles, laughter and back slapping in their pleasure of seeing one another again. His friend asked, "Who's Seasick Sylvester?"

Dick said, "It's me. I was sick as a dog all the way across the Atlantic and if I hadn't known Major Bomar (referring to me) was waiting for me, I couldn't have made it. I upchucked the whole damned way."

His buddy hobbled on crutches. His left foot and leg were in a cast up to the knee. He and Dick were genuinely pleased to see a familiar face in a crowd of strangers. He sat down with his plastered leg poking out in one direction; Dick sat with his bandaged leg poking out in another and told him about the horrible storm at sea.

"The weather was so severe, the Seminole got lost. We had no means of communication. No sense of direction. The captain went on deck and something knifed him in the jugular."

"Did it kill him?"

Dick shared the good news. "No. He was lucky. He had immediate access to the finest medical attention." Naturally! He was on a hospital ship!

Holleran General was a stop-over for many of the men. The wartime policy required all wounded servicemen to go to a hospital in their home state and since Dick was from Tennessee, he was assigned to the orthopedic clinic at Kennedy

General in Memphis; a huge hospital with three thousand patients.

At the end of our three days at Holleran, there was a mass migration of the wounded; all the men, who had been brought back to the states on the Seminole. Dick was assigned the position of Trainmaster, putting him in charge of all those going to Tennessee. With this responsibility, he left directly from the hospital so he could supervise the men. He had to see to it that the men got into the hospital vans which were ferried to Manhattan and had to check them off when they boarded the train to Memphis. I had the responsibility of cleaning up the apartment.

I was anxious that everything be in order for the nurse, who had been kind enough to let us use her place and I was nervous about getting Dick's and my things together and making it to the train on time.

To this day, I can't explain it. Somehow, somebody led me astray.

I didn't get settled in the train good before the conductor cried, "All aboard!" The wheels started rolling and we were on our way.

I asked the smiling, black conductor where the servicemen were who had just boarded. "I'm looking for my husband, Major Bomar, and a number of men who are being transferred to Memphis."

"Lady, I ain't seen no soldiers goin' to Memphis, cause we ain't goin' to Memphis. We's goin' to Nashville."

"Nashville!" I screamed.

"Lady, I think you done made a mistake."

Harsh reality set in. "Oh, Lord! I'm on the wrong train!"

The conductor was not helpful. "It's gonna take a spell to git there. There's some pretty scenery along the way. Might as well sit back and enjoy the ride."

I didn't enjoy the ride. I sat there and fumed and stewed like a tea kettle ready to blow its whistle, til I decided to get off at Bell Buckle, call Dick's parents and ask them for sanctuary.

Of all the rotten things to happen! I was trapped! Headed for Nashville, while my so recently reacquainted husband made his way to Memphis without me. Getting on the wrong plane or train is not the same as making the wrong exit from an expressway. You have to sit there until the vehicle gets where its going. And there I stayed through the day and through the night til we came to Bell Buckle the following day.

Dick's parents were surprised to hear from me, but were nice as they could be. They met me at the train station in Bell Buckle and when we arrived at their home, Mr. Bomar placed a phone call to Dick. When he got through to him, Dick's father asked him if he had lost anything. Mr. Bomar had a nice sense of humor.

Dick, who had learned in a little over two years, not to be surprised at whatever I might do, said he was pleased to know my whereabouts. And the train mix-up had a happy ending, because Dick got a leave to be with his family for a few days and we had a nice visit in the peace and quiet of Bell Buckle with his mom and dad.

Dick's parents were shocked to see how much weight he had lost and the condition of his hand. Fortunately, it wasn't as smelly as it had been when he first arrived on the hospital ship, but it still looked bad. The bandage covered most of his arm and it was painful. And the wound in his leg, although it wasn't as noticeable, gave him a lot of trouble. He had a bad limp.

Mr. and Mrs. Bomar wanted to be sure their son had the best care available and I tried to convince them that, as a registered nurse, I would see to it that he got it. Dick's father had a strong political contact and while we were in Bell Buckle, he made several phone calls to try to help his son by pulling a few strings. As a result, I was allowed to nurse Dick at Kennedy General for the entire sixteen months he was there.

I went back into uniform, acted as Dick's private nurse and watched over him and nursed him through seven operations.

The first operation was a delicate, tedious one, which lasted nearly five hours. Following the surgery, even though they kept him sedated, the pain was excruciating. I knew I needed to be with him and had an orderly to bring in one of the hospital portable stretchers and I slept in the room with him for the next few days.

It was not the best of all possible worlds. The guests on either side of Dick's room didn't think it was such a hot idea either. In order to get as close as possible, I tied my little portable bed-on-wheels to Dick's bed with long rolls of cotton bandage. My efforts were not satisfactory.

With the least movement, my bed on wheels came loose and I shot across the room, banging into the wall.

The third night of this arrangement, a nurse passed by in the hall at the moment of impact. She quietly opened the door, peered into the semi-darkness and inquired, "Mrs. Bomar, is there a problem?"

For all she might have known, where I landed was where I was supposed to be and I didn't want to get into any trouble, so I said in a sleepy voice as if she had just awakened me, "Thank you. Everything's fine," I lied.

It was definitely not the best of times.

I hadn't had a decent night's sleep in days. The patients in the adjacent rooms complained about the sudden loud noises in the middle of the night. It was particularly rough for the guy on the other side of the wall where I crash landed several times a night.

He called the nurse and yelled: "What the hell's going on here?" There's so much racket going on, I thought I was back in the war zone!

"Yes, sir. The private nurse in the next room seems to be having a problem. Let me see what I can do."

"Tell 'em to pipe down!"

Dick was groggy from sedation and the commotion next door didn't register. Still, it was embarrassing. I had heard. I confided in the floor nurse and when she realized what was going on, she offered to help. She tried her hand with a knot she was sure would hold the two beds together. It did; for about an hour.

Although Dick generally had a good sense of humor and had become stoic about a lot of things, if he started to doze off with me stretched out by his side and all of a sudden I careened across the room, it did nothing to improve his out-look on life.

Chapter 30
THE HEALING PROCESS

A few days later, when Dick was feeling stronger, I found a cute little two-bedroom house close by.

The house was owned by a lady, whose husband was overseas. She let us have it with the provision that she could use one of the bedrooms from time to time. It wasn't the best arrangement, but it was hard to find a place during the war, so we took it. It had a nice curb appeal and on the inside, there was a living room, dinette, kitchen, two bedrooms and one bath, which made it rather cozy, when the owner was there, but she traveled and was seldom at home.

This was where we stayed between surgery.

All of the operations on Dick's hand were hard on him. I remember a particularly long one when he had a tendon transplant. After this procedure, Dick went in and out of shock and it scared me to death. With his susceptibility to shock, I became concerned about one particular drug.

Sulfa diozene was a new 'miracle' drug the doctors had just started using and because it was so new, they hadn't learned how to gauge the dosage properly. I found out that a number of patients had gotten a bad reaction from the drug and I was worried about Dick taking it.

Fortunately, I kept close watch on him and when the doctor said he wanted to try this new drug on Dick, I gave him only half the amount the doctor prescribed. I wanted to see how he would react to it.

Within minutes, Dick started turning blue. I yelled to the nurses and told them to get the oxygen tank to Dick's room STAT! The nurses went into action and I was so frantic, I screamed the whole time they were coming down the hall! A few minutes later, the color started to return to his face and I was so relieved, I broke down, which is something I don't ordinarily do anymore.

I thought I had lost him.

I'd been in hospitals enough to know that accidents do happen and I didn't want Dick to be the victim of anybody's carelessness.

Hospitals have their share of personnel problems just like any other place. The only difference is that in a hospital, what you do or don't do may frequently mean the difference between a live patient and a dead one. I had good cause to be concerned at Kennedy General on only this one occasion.

At the nurses' station near Dick's room, there was a dear, sweet, older nurse, who frequently fell asleep and failed to answer the calls from the patients. This little lady was one of those unfortunate souls, who succumb to the availability of drugs and get hooked on them. She had been on duty the night Dick started turning blue and if I hadn't been there, he wouldn't have made it. She left the hospital not long after the emergency with Dick. I never knew exactly what happened about her dismissal. I felt sorry for her, but I knew she had no business being there.

Because I wore a white uniform, everybody thought I was an army nurse and I made a lot of friends among the hospital personnel, in addition to the nurse who tried to help me when I was bunking in Dick's room. The Chief Nurse was impressed with the way I worked and from time to time, I helped out and took on extra responsibilities.

There were a couple of young nurses, who liked to take off on the weekend and whenever this happened, I took over the floor and looked after forty patients. There was no extra pay; I just did it.

During this period, I often bathed eight patients every morning. It was hard work. And it was heartbreaking. Some of the wounded soldiers were in such terrible condition, with missing arms, or legs, or parts of the face, or body. One man had an awful wound in the stomach. He didn't live long. Another one had been hit in the crotch and wanted to die. One man had lost one arm and both legs. This man had the greatest courage to survive of any patient I have ever nursed. When my heart was bleeding for the men and the tears so close to the surface, I thought, "How dare I break down in front of these brave men, who are looking to me for comfort!" And somehow, I kept going.

Faced with the grim realty of war everyday, it was necessary to break the strain with periods of diversion. And as Dick improved, we visited the other patients, who were well enough to enjoy company. Sometimes we strolled around the grounds of this huge hospital or walked up and down the halls.

Sometimes, we went to a room, where there was an old upright piano and I played and sang, along with those who wanted to join in on the popular wartime songs, some of the classic oldies, or hymns that everybody knew. Sometimes, we just sat and talked and laughed and swapped stories with one another.

We met some nice people at Kennedy General. When you're in one hospital for over a year, you get to know a lot of folks, if you're outgoing like Dick and I both were.

Dick was puny when we first got there, but as the months went by, his strength returned, particularly after he started playing golf. And we ended up having some nice memories of our stay at Kennedy General. We made a few friendships which have lasted a lifetime.

For the entire time Dick was stationed at Kennedy General, during the periods between operations, he was required to report each day from nine to five and I went with him, just as if we were going to work together. In a sense, we were. It was a challenge for both of us to get through Dick's ordeal.

Dick's orthopedic surgeon was Major Flanigan, a long lanky redheaded Irishman. He looked to be about six three and when he spoke, you knew you'd been spoken to. He didn't take any foolishness from Dick or any other patients. When he told you to do something; you did it. Dr.

Flanigan had a sharp sense of humor. He'd seen so much, he needed it. Dick needed it, too.

For a while after we arrived at Kennedy Hospital, on some days, Dick was as low as he could get. He would get discouraged and felt like he'd never get the use of his hand again, and in the back of his mind was the constant fear he'd never be able to fly again. That thought made him feel like his situation was more than he could cope with. Dr. Flanigan was a compassionate man, but he frequently barked at Dick, when he started feeling too sorry for himself.

He told Dick, "You're a mighty lucky man to have such a lovely nurse to take care of you." And he teased, "It is necessary that you pay attention to Mrs. Bomar and do exactly what she tells you to do." All concerned knew what he was referring to. He had given Dick a set of little exercises he was supposed to do each day. They were tedious. They were hard and they were painful. Dick hated them and even though I tried to make him do them, he often rebelled. He was also known to yell, "I'm not going to do them!"

Dick's bad attitude was noted on his chart and one day when Major Flanigan saw it, he tore into Dick and read the riot act.

"Major Bomar! You are to do those exercises everyday! You are to do what Mrs. Bomar tells you to do and I don't want any more rebellion out of you! Here we are trying to give you a second chance with your hand. And you're acting like a school boy, who doesn't want to do his lessons!"

Dick interjected a meek, "Yes, sir." And the doctor continued his loud tirade.

"Furthermore, if you don't do your exercises as I've instructed you to do, you may never get back the use of your hand!" He knew of Dick's goal to fly again, and landed a verbal jolt in his solar plexus. "You do want to fly again, don't you?" With this soul-searing question, he stormed out.

He never had to fuss at Dick again. I never held it against Major Flanigan. If he hadn't been as strict as he was, Dick might never have recovered the use of his hand.

One of the worse days came when the doctor decided it would be good therapy for him to learn how to knit, to give a gentle exercise to his hand.

Dick hit the ceiling.

He yelled, "Not on your life! Knitting is for sissies! I'm not going to do it!"

I said, "Yes you are going to do it."

Major Flanigan said firmly, "Yes you are going to do it!" And Dick did it.

The result was an unforgettable, unfortunate-looking scarf; the product of his creativity under duress, and it showed. The "Thing", as he called it, was an olive drab color, which was enough to get it off to a bad start, with no redeeming feature. There was no chance of that ugly duckling emerging into a graceful swan. The therapist, a large, dark woman, with no sense of humor and no tact, tried to show Dick the basic knit-one-purl-one stockinet stitch.

"Major Bomar, even small children and the mentally insane are able to knit. I'm sure you can master it."

Dick mumbled something about the monotony of knitting being enough to drive anybody crazy. But he tried.

The therapist got him started on a scarf that was twelve inches wide and it grew and grew, while Dick exercised his hand. It was an unusual piece of apparel. The stitches were uneven. There were occasional holes, where none were supposed to be, and what should have been a plain, smooth surface developed into a strange-looking pattern and the 'Thing' became the topic of conversation among all who saw it. Dick's fame spread throughout the hospital and drew curiosity seekers from other floors. Eventually, his snappish behavior subsided as he began to derive a certain pleasure displaying his creation.

Major Flanigan was pleased and encouraged Dick about his knitting. He said, "I'm very proud of you, Major Bomar." And rolled his R's so that he almost sounded like he was purring.

When the scarf grew to some twelve feet, the therapist pronounced the project a success and Dick was released from his labor.

Chapter 31
LIFE AT KENNEDY GENERAL HOSPITAL

I found it to be an interesting experience taking care of Dick at Kennedy General. There's a different atmosphere between a civilian hospital and a military one. Kennedy was decidedly military. You felt it the minute you entered the door. It extended into the furthermost reaches of the building. It was a good feeling; that awareness of being under the aegis of the United States Armed Forces. And with the feeling of protection, came certain rules and regulations not found in non-military hospitals. For example, people are not expected to salute a civilian hospital administrator. However, the servicemen in a military hospital are expected to salute the military counterpart, the Chief of Staff.

This bit of military protocol was so deeply ingrained in Dick, he tried to observe it even when he was physically unable. One time it gave us a good laugh.

After one of his operations, he was still groggy from the anesthesia when the Chief of Staff made his rounds to look in on the patients. If possible, you were supposed to be fully dressd, including a tie. You were supposed to stand. You were supposed to salute. It also helped if you were in your right mind. At the time, Dick could not adequately fulfill any of these requisites, but when the Colonel briskly entered the room, Dick tried valiantly to stand. I knew he was still too heavily sedated to get up and from across the room, I looked in horror as he tried to rise. I dashed to assist him. Too late! His legs buckled and he fell over backwards on the bed, with his hand in an upside down salute.

The Colonel congratulated him on his effort.

After he left, almost in a whisper, Dick said, "I may not have been on my feet, Birdie, but I did salute him." And the sedation carried him back to dreamland where he belonged.

The Chief Nurse at Kennedy General was also a colonel: Colonel Mahar, a scrupulously neat-looking, small, brown-haired woman, somewhere in her mid forties; the epitome of efficiency. She gave the impression she knew everything going on all over the hospital. She knew I was a registered nurse and that I was looking after my husband. She knew the demands on the staff nurses were difficult and she welcomed my presence. She also knew I had been helping a couple of nurses on several occasions.

We hadn't had much contact with one another, but one day as I got ready to make my daily trek to the officer's club for lunch, she approached me.

"Mrs. Bomar, you are not only providing a fine service for Major Bomar, you are also a help to the other nurses on the floor. I know it's hard on you going out to eat everyday and I want to make arrangements for you to eat in the nurses' dining room on this floor. It'll save you time and money."

I was delighted. I could surely use all the extra time and money I could get.

I've always been able to get along with people and generally make friends easily. Colonel Mahar and I hit it off fine. She seemed to like me, respected my knowledge about nursing and hospital work and not long after, she asked me if I would fill in for the Head Nurse on Dick's floor, who wanted to be with her family on Christmas day. I was glad to do this, because Dick and I would be there anyway and with the experience I had as Assistant Night Supervisor at South Highland, I felt confident I could handle any situation which might arise.

Christmas Eve, Dick and I had a quiet little celebration in his room. I fixed up a small Christmas tree and placed a couple of gifts under it for Dick to open in the morning. I made my rounds. Just before supper, a choir from one of the local churches came by and sang Christmas carols. The dietician outdid herself with a good meal and there was the prospect of turkey and dressing with all the trimmings tomorrow. We tuned in a radio comedy and got a few laughs. Later in the evening, we had a station softly playing Christmas music in the background and Dick was in a good frame of mind. Everything had been so quiet, I was able to spend the better part of the evening with Dick. It was as nice a Christmas Eve as you could expect to have in a hospital.

This was just before things in the mental ward went haywire.

Dick started nodding off and I left his room to get a fresh pitcher of water. Immediately, I saw a pale-faced young nurse come running toward me down the hall. She looked frantic.

"Quick! We need you in Section Eight!"

I knew Section Eight was the mental ward on the next floor down. It didn't frighten me. I'd had experience with loonies before. I asked what kind of shenanigans were going on. She told me.

"One of the patients is drunk and pulling teeth like crazy! Get your ward boy and come!"

I quickly found the ward boy in a small supply room and shouted, "Junior! Come with me!" Junior was well trained. When a nurse spoke like that, he knew to drop everything and go. Junior (not his real name) was a big, strapping young black man, strong as a bull and looked like he could subdue anybody.

We took the fastest way down the stairs to Section Eight and ran toward a room where we heard a lot of commotion. There were shouts, laughter and clapping. The closer we got, the louder it became.

I opened the door and saw a large bald-headed man dancing around in his pajamas in the middle of the ward, holding a pair of pliers high over his head. Clasped in the pliers was somebody's tooth. He wore a tinsel crown with a bright red ribbon drooping down over one ear. He looked like he was in some sort of ecstatic trance.

One patient was bending over a basin spitting out blood. Another, in a corner, was groaning and holding a blood-spotted cloth against his mouth. Several men on the sidelines were shouting, chanting some mumbo-jumbo, clapping and egging on the frantic dance of the man, who was the self-proclaimed dentist. A quiet, frail-looking man stood at the head of a small line and looked like the next victim. The rest of those in the ward were propped up on their beds enjoying the sideshow, in varying states of awareness.

Caught up in the emotion of the moment, the bogus dentist whirled around in another world.

I whispered to Junior, "Grab him! And don't let go til I get a straight-jacket!"

Immediately, one of the floor nurses handed over the needed garment.

The pretender was big, but Junior was bigger and in no time, he had the 'dentist' under control.

He protested mightily with a thick tongue. "Whut're you doin' this for? I'm jus tryin' to help! These payshens need my attenshun. I'm the medicine man! I'm a dentish and I'm p'formin' a service."

I asked, "Are you a licensed dentist?"

"Yes, officer."

I ignored the title. "Did you make a habit of doing a war dance after each extraction?"

He didn't answer. Junior led him away.

The room became dead silent. The men standing on the sidelines became statues; slightly weaving statues. I looked at them and knew at once that they had been imbibing along with Buddy. Somehow, liquor had made its way into the requisite tee totalling Section Eight.

I scanned the room and saw a nicely decorated, uncut cake, covered with cherries and a bright red "Merry Christmas" message on top. Next to it, lying on its side, was an empty liquor bottle. On closer investigation, I saw that the cake was a fake. It was an ingenious shell, designed to camouflage a large bottle of gin.

Some misguided friend had wanted Buddy, the medicine man, and his pals to have a little enjoyment out of life, without realizing that one of the most dangerous combustible combinations is a "fruit cake" mixed with alcohol.

I learned later that Buddy had always been like a big teddy bear. He was simply one of those, who lose touch with reality with one good size drink inside the belly.

After everybody had been subdued and Buddy had been sent off to dry out and the unfortunate men who had been operated on had received a little attention, I asked the nurses in Section Eight where on earth Buddy could have gotten the pliers.

I hung around while they summoned the maintenance man. He identified the tool as his.

When Colonel Mahar heard about the incident, the fur flew. The maintenance man flew further. He was never heard of again.

* * * * * * *

Dick's physician told him it was important for him to keep busy, not only for the sake of his morale, but also to exercise his hand to help strengthen it. The doctor felt that Dick had passed the knitting stage. He knew Dick didn't like to play cards, which some patients did, and one day in a joking mood, he told Dick, "You have a choice. You can either play cards or play golf." He knew good and well what Dick's choice would be and he added, "If you want to play golf, I'll have one of the therapists go with you to the golf course."

With the option of playing either cards or golf, golf won by a long shot.

Filled with considerable enthusiasm, Dick and I made our way down to Beal Street to a little pawnshop we'd heard about and bought a few clubs and some kind of old cloth golf bag. Dick had never played golf and he found the prospect exciting; something of an adventure after the depressing atmosphere of the hospital. He considered himself lucky, when he thought of all the wounded servicemen, who would never be able to play golf, or much of anything else.

The therapist took us to a golf course not far away. It was owned by Mr. Cox (I'm not sure if that's his name.) He was also the instructor and what with the therapist giving pointers and Mr. Cox adding his two cents worth, Dick had plenty of attention. We hit it off right away with Mr. Cox, and while I tagged along during the lessons, I talked with him and told him how much I wished I could learn to play, so Dick and I could play together.

That turned out to be my lucky day. Mr. Cox told us about a girl, who had been taking golf lessons from him. She was going to California with her husband, who had been transferred. Mr. Cox was designated to sell her clubs.

I asked, "How much?"

"Twenty bucks. They're an expensive matched set. It's a steal!"

I looked at Dick. He gave a nod and I said joyfully, "I'll take 'em!" So I became the proud owner of a fine set of golf clubs, while Dick's came from the pawnshop. But, he didn't mind and he turned out to be a crackerjack player. And I didn't do too badly myself.

Dick still had to go for therapy sessions every morning at the hospital, but as soon as we could catch an early noon meal, we headed for the golf course. We played every day, Monday through Friday, when it wasn't raining and Dick started to come to life, like he hadn't been since he returned from overseas. He put on weight. The color returned to his face and he started to look like the old Dick I'd known before he went off to war.

When Dick's doctor finally told him, he'd done all he could do and the time to leave had arrived, it was hard to believe we'd been there so long. Sixteen months had passed and Dick had survived seven operations.

Just before he left Kennedy General, he had a visitor, who offered him the encouragement he so badly needed.

He and I were in his room, when there was a knock at the door. Dick said, "Come in." And in walked Captain Eddie Rickenbacker, the famous World War One hero and head of Eastern Airlines. We could scarcely believe it! Here was this fabled man, who downed twenty-six enemy planes and collected nineteen decorations for bravery, including the Congressional Medal of Honor.

Here in Dick's room was Eddie Rickenbacker! The man, who crash-landed in the Pacific and guided his crew during a twenty-four day struggle for survival.

He was a tall, fine looking man; a man of physical strength, with big bushy, dark eyebrows and warm compassionate eyes. A man, known for his strength of character and firm religious conviction. Dick and I rose when he came in.

He greeted both of us; walked over to Dick and held out his hand.

"Major, men like you are always needed by Eastern. I want you to know, there's a job waiting for you, whether you can fly again, or not. Let us hear from you as soon as you can. We'll be waiting." He paused, while he reached in his pocket for an envelope. He handed it to Dick.

"Major, I want to personally commend you for the fine manner in which you have served your country and this is a small token of appreciation for your work at Eastern." It was a bonus of seventy-five dollars. Seventy-five dollars was a lot more then than it is now. It was a much-needed bonus, which we could certainly put to good use.

I was afraid Dick was going to choke up with emotion when he saluted his former employer and said, "Thank, you." A photographer took a picture of them. I still have a copy somewhere.

Dick and I were both impressed that this famous man had taken his valuable time to visit a former pilot with Eastern. It did worlds of good for Dick's morale. It was not a case of his feeling inadequate. He never doubted his knowledge of flying and his ability to be a good pilot. He simply knew that his left hand would always be weak for the rest of his life. He knew he could cope with a desk job and it was good to know that one would be waiting for him, but even if it allowed him to make a living and keep occupied, he knew he'd never be happy with it. He wanted to fly and that's what he was determined to do.

Dick was sent to Miami to be reassigned for temporary duty. During the two weeks it took to complete this process, we stayed at the Whitman Hotel; a beautiful place on the beach, where we lived in luxury for seventy-five cents a day. From Miami we were sent to Stout Field, in Indianapolis, for six months temporary duty, where the doctors would determine whether or not Dick could pilot a plane again. There was some indecision, so Dick was sent for further examination and opinion from a specialist at Fort Benjamin Harrison Hospital, which was also in Indianapolis. This is where Dick received his disability discharge.

The doctor looked at Dick's hand and said, "I'm sorry, Major. Your hand injury will not allow you to continue flying in the Air Force."

Dick was hurt to the core.

"Do you think it functions well enough for me to go back to flying for Eastern?"

"I can't answer that, Major. Piloting a commercial aircraft is not as difficult as piloting in combat. The demands made on a pilot's muscular coordination in a war zone are much greater. It can mean the difference between life and death, not only for you, but for countless others." I started to mention that a commercial pilot also held the lives of others in his hands. Instead Dick asked, "You think I have a chance?"

"That will be up to the examining physicians for the FAA and Eastern. Good luck."

Dick separated from the Air Force and we returned to Atlanta July 7, 1945. He never went back into regular service after he was wounded.

At the time we returned to Atlanta, my sister Lema was working with Delta and when we told her we were coming home, we asked her to help us find a home to rent and she found a beautiful one for us out on the Old Jonesboro Road. Within a few days, Dick wanted to get things moving. He was eager to get back his old job with Eastern.

With considerable apprehension, Dick went through the required Federal Aeronautic Association examination. When the doctor checked out Dick's hand, he noted the wounded left arm was shorter than the other. He said, "If you can play the piano, you can fly."

Dick replied, "I don't play the piano. Birdie does that. How about the trumpet? Or the jug? Would that help?"

The doctor had no sense of humor and was non-committal. I'll add here that later I did teach Dick how to play the piano. He also learned to play the Hammond Organ, which I think I mentioned earlier.

The examination was extensive. Dick said he felt like they'd looked over every inch of his body with a magnifying glass, inside and out. He passed the FAA physical and we both breathed a sigh of relief. He had passed phase one.

Phase two lay ahead.

Chapter 32
THE RETURN TO CIVILIAN LIFE

When Dick passed the FAA physical, he knew he was on his way. Eastern required all of its pilots to pass a physical, but he felt since he had been able to pass the very demanding FAA examination, the company test would be a snap. He was right.

He passed it; maybe not with flying colors, since there was no disguising the damage, which had been done to his hand and leg, but the examining physician at the headquarters in Miami pronouced him in good enough condition to return to his old job. Eastern was ready to trust him with its planes, and more importantly, with the safety of its passengers.

Dick was ecstatic. There had been so many long months, when he doubted that he would ever fly again.

He started back to work at Eastern as a co-pilot and was required to go through a three-month training period in Miami, before being promoted to Captain. This was understandable. He had been away from commercial flight for nearly two years. These few months in Miami were a happy time for both of us. Dick did what he loved best: flying. And I did what I loved best: taking care of Dick. In many ways, I guess this was one of the most relaxed periods of my life. I was happy among people I enjoyed being with. We stayed in a lovely room in a beachfront hotel. We went out for all our meals and with no cooking and no housekeeping, I adapted quickly to the role of a lady of leisure.

Lema, who was able to get passes through Delta, came down a couple of times. The last time, she brought Lorraine, her roommate. It turned out to be a weekend none of us would ever forget.

It started out in such a normal, routine way. Dick had just come in from a flight. We were sitting around talking, trying to decide what to do that evening; wondering if we ought to brave the elements, since the weather had started getting rough.

The phone rang. It was Elsie Bennett, my former roommate and the current secretary of Captain Sid Shannon, vice-president in charge of operations at Eastern. She extended an enthusiastic invitation. She said Captain and Mrs. Shannon had gone to Virginia for a few days and had turned over their beautiful bay front home to her and several other folks with Eastern.

The effusive invitation had a motive behind it. Elsie knew I was a nurse and she thought I'd be a good person to have around, because one of the guests was very pregnant; like ready to deliver any minute. The mother-to-be was Nedra Coleman, Captain Eddie Rickenbacker's niece. Nedra was past due and big as a barrel. She had no business being there, but how do you say "no" to the niece of Captain Rickenbacker? With a storm brewing, she should have been inland, close to her husband and a hospital, but she wanted to stay, so Elsie decided she'd like to have me close by in case of an emergency, when I would take on the responsibility of a midwife.

The invitation had to include Lema and Lorraine.

This made no difference to Elsie. She yelled into the phone, "Y'all come on down and wait out the storm with us! There's plenty of room!

There's plenty of food! Y'all come on as quick as you can. If Nedra's baby decides to come in the middle of the storm and we can't get out, it'll be awful. You've got to come!"

I considered the consequences. "That's all I need! To have a baby come in the middle of a hurricane!"

Elsie disregarded my concern. "Park the car in back of the house. It'll be more protected there. And come on! It's getting breezy down here!"

Within half an hour, Dick, Lema, Lorraine and I piled in our new car and were on our way.

The Shannons had a gorgeous home overlooking the bay; a handsome large structure, with lovely professionally landscaped grounds. By the time we got there, the palm trees were swaying in a strong wind and a couple of times, the thought passed my mind that we were a bunch of idiots to take off in such bad weather. I had serious doubts about wanting the glory attached to delivering a baby in the middle of a storm, but we were young and foolish and thought a hurricane party was a fun thing to do.

Elsie, Nedra, plus an old friend and her husband gave us a hearty welcome and I made light of the situation.

"Hi! We just blew in for a hurricane party!"

That evening, while the storm was developing out at sea, everything went along well. We sat around and talked about people we knew and the experiences we'd had since we last saw one another. Dick told some stories abut his experiences overseas. We had a radio to listen to music and weather reports. We also had an advantage over other people in the area. Nedra's husband was a meteorologist with the U. S. Weather Bureau. He had to work that weekend, but he called at regular intervals to give us the latest reports and to check on how his wife and child-to-be were doing.

In 1945, practically nobody had television; not even at the Shannons' beach house. VCRs didn't exist. Neither did video games. We listened to the wartime favorite records on a big floor model phonograph player and turned on radio news and weather reports. Some of the gang played cards. And Elsie and I cooked. And cooked.

On Saturday, the wind calmed down. We were able to get outside. The men battened down the windows as best they could and the women walked on the beach.

The Shannons' home was beautifully furnished. It provided a breath-taking view of the bay. If the weather hadn't acted up, it would have been an ideal vacation retreat. It had a large kitchen with a very large stove. The pantry was stocked with cans and packages of food and in addition to a huge refrigerator, there was a giant-size freezer, chock full of frozen fish, meat, chicken, fruits and vegetables and a bunch of frozen delicacies for dessert and snacking. The Shannons were prepared so there wouldn't have to be extra trips made to the grocery store. A well-stocked bar was available for anybody who wanted it. Nobody used it. We had sense enough to realize we could be heading into trouble and wanted to be alert. This was not your typical hurricane party with everybody sitting around getting snookered as the wind increased in velocity. It's bad enough to hang around when the elements are out of control. Trying to cope with the danger of a giant storm rolling in across the bay with a hangover is just plain dumb. Those of us who had flown through storms respected the unpredictable power of the elements.

Sunday afternoon, the rain started and the wind began to moan. Nedra passed along a pearl of wisdom, courtesy of a distant relative, who said, "When the wind starts talking, you know the storm is near."

It must have been around three P. M., when the electricity went off. That meant no radio and no record playing. This didn't bother us too much. We could do without the music. The radio reception had gotten so bad, it was pure static and we felt sure the refrigerated and frozen food would keep, if the current didn't stay off too long.

At four o'clock, the phone still worked. Nedra's husband warned us that the storm would strike within the next couple of hours. We felt prepared.

The sky had been overcast with a depressing, dull gray haze all day and it started getting darker. The rain came down harder. In the distance, we could hear deep rumbling thunder. An occasional flash lit up the sky. Elsie and I scurried around looking for candles to ward off the gloom. And all of us paid extra attention to Nedra, trying to keep her calm. The thought of her having her baby in the middle of a hurricane didn't appeal to anybody, especially me, because I knew I'd be carrying the full responsibility.

Without the use of the radio and record player, we were left to our own ingenuity to keep entertained. Elsie and I had cooked enough to keep us going for a couple of days. It would have been a waste to spend more time in the kitchen.

Nobody wanted to play cards. Or chess. Or checkers. Charades seemed silly.

We started getting cabin fever.

In the midst of our restlessness, Joe, (not his real name) the only other man in the group, got a crazy notion that could have been disastrous for all of us. It's amazing how an ordinarily sane, well-balanced person can sometimes develop a loose screw on short notice.

He piped up. "I think I'll take a walk outside to see what's happening in the neighborhood."

His wife yelled, "Joe, you're crazy!"

His motive was noble, he thought. "I just want to see if there are any lost souls, who need help."

Dick kept a clear head. He warned, "I don't think I'd do that, Joe."

"Yeah, well, I think I'd like to go and find out if anybody else has electricity."

I put in my two cents. "You're nuts! It's dangerous for you to go walking outside in this weather. You won't even be able to stand up!"

Some people are born mule-headed. At that moment, Joe was one of them.

He opened the door and nearly blew the place away. He not only nearly blew it away, he came close to causing a serious fire.

When he opened the door, he got more than he bargained for. The velocity of the wind knocked him off his feet. He couldn't close the door. Dick and a couple of others dashed across the room, pushed the door shut and secured it with the burglar chain. And everybody was so busy watching them trying to close the door, nobody noticed that a candle on the mantle had toppled over in the gale, landed on a stack of papers by the fireplace and ignited them. Before we knew what was happening, the flames flared up to the ceiling.

Elsie screamed, "Oh, my God! The place is on fire!"

I ran to the kitchen and brought back a pitcher of water to douse the flames. No serious damage was done, but it shook us up when we realized how quickly the flames grew and what a narrow escape we had. Joe was also shaken and quickly returned to a guilt-stricken state of awareness.

It took a while to get things back in order and when it was all over, we were relieved that we didn't have to replace any furnishings. If those papers had burned anywhere else in the house, it would have been a different story, and a very costly vacation for all of us.

Nedra, who hadn't done anything in particular, except get herself worked up over all the excitement, collapsed on the sofa and then we had her to worry about.

From then on, things got progressively worse. Sharp flashes of lightning brought an eerie momentary brightness, followed so closely by deafening jolts of thunder, we knew we were now in the midst of the storm. The rain swirled down in sheets and lashed against the house. You could tell from the sound the sand was mixed with the water and Dick started to worry about our new car. It should have been light at six o'clock; the sky was a forbidding dark gray. We couldn't see the car from the house and even if we could have, it wouldn't have done any good. The wind howled around the house making eerie noises. It was scary.

The men had battened down the windows on the first floor earlier, but I didn't think it would give us the protection we needed. The Shannon home was very modern for its time and had lots of glass. There was no way we could get it all covered.

Everybody tried to carry on a conversation, however trite, or make weak jokes over what was happening. Lema sat there like she was transfixed and never said a word. Elsie and I made some sandwiches and set them out on the table. Nobody cared. When you're scared half out of your wits you're going to be washed away by a tidal wave, it cuts your appetite, especially if you're sober. And there was nobody to blame, because we had all asked for it.

As the storm swelled, we knew what it must be like to be inside a washing machine.

The wind-swept water continued its frenzied assault and in the semi-darkness, we could barely see the palm trees in the front yard. They were bending almost to the ground, with their branches looking like long hair blowing in the wind and rain and sand.

And the noises were nerve-wracking. It sounded like we were in a war zone. Unknown objects crashed around us. A number of strange sounding thuds pummeled the side of the house. We were being bombarded.

Dick tried to add a touch of levity to the tense situation. "I've flown through worse storms than this."

There were some exasperated sighs and groans. Tempers were getting edgy. I decided to break away from the group.

I always loved storms. I liked the excitement. I knew there were some windows that hadn't been boarded on the second floor and I bolted up the stairs to get another view of this wild phenomenon. When I was a little over half way up, Dick yelled, "Birdie, come here! It's not safe up there!"

At the top of the stairs, I stopped abruptly.

In the front bedroom, in the pale eerie light, something moved. I knew everybody was downstairs and I nearly jumped out of my skin.

I screamed, "Dick! You come here!"

As my eyes became accustomed to the dim light, I saw the rug levitating. It was the strangest sight I've ever seen.

The four by six rug hovered several inches off the floor by the side of the bed. It performed a crazy kind of floating dance.

I screamed again, "Dick!"

Everybody except Nedra bounded up the stairs.

Dick sized up the situation in a split second. "Calm down, Birdie. It's nothing. It's from pressure cause by the storm. The air pressure is so strong, it's causing the rug to rise."

We watched the performance, spellbound for a few seconds and broke out in nervous laughter; laughter that helped to ease the tension.

At the height of the storm, the phone went dead while Nedra talked with her husband. That was our last contact with the outside world. Nedra panicked. She was sure her labor pains had started. I took her back to her bedroom where she could be quiet; made her lie down and put some cold cloths on her forehead and brewed a pot of hot tea. In about thirty minutes, the panic passed.

Heavy rain continued into the evening and was still going strong, when we went to bed. The next morning, we went outside and surveyed the destruction.

Debris was everywhere. The sky was overcast and a strange calmness filled the air. From the top of one of the palm trees in the yard, a man's blue shirt was flapping gently like some strange looking flag, blown in from heaven knows where. Broken pieces of driftwood were strewn as far as we could see. A mangled small metal umbrella table leaned against the side of the house; its umbrella nowhere in sight. I was thankful it had landed there instead of trying to go through a door or window. A twisted tricycle with a few patches of red paint still visible sat on the lawn. A sopping wet, small bedraggled-looking oriental rug weighted down the shrubbery. It was a far cry from its dancing cousin we had enjoyed the night before.

Our car had gone belly up. One side had been bashed in and it was a mess. It looked like it had been sandblasted. Sand was everywhere! A small barbecue grill had crashed against the front windshield. Wet, smelly sand banked up on one side of the interior. The exterior looked like it had never seen a coat of paint. Our beautiful new car we had been so proud of was a total wreck.

We were dazed from the experience, but we were all safe.

We had made it through the storm. We found that our neighbors had made it. And Nedra's baby had stayed put until we could get her back to her relieved husband. We had a lot to be thankful for.

The sun broke through the haze and it seemed so strange, looking at the destruction around us, thinking how different it was in the calm peaceful sunshine, remembering the anxiety we had known the night before. The sky looked as innocent and placid as if it had never happened.

A few days after the storm, Dick was transferred from Miami to Atlanta. We got rid of the car and gathered our things together.

We said goodbye to the good friends we'd made and looked forward to a new beginning far removed from the horrors of war; a new beginning of a relationship built on a sure foundation of faith, and a love, which we hoped would believe all things, bear all things and endure all things.

Wishful thinking? Sure it was. But we were young and ready to give it a try.

When we boarded the plane to return to Atlanta, I turned around to say something and inadvertently poked Dick in the eye with the long feather in my hat. That was part of what Dick had to endure.

While we were waiting for take-off, thunder rumbled faintly in the distance. Always ready for adventure, I looked at Dick and said hopefully, "Maybe we'll see some Saint Elmos's fire," and caught a glimpse of a twinkle in his eye.

As we became airborne, it started to rain.

EPILOGUE

William Richard Bomar was awarded the Purple Heart; Air Medal; the European-African-Middle Eastern Theatre Ribbon with two Stars, and the American Theatre Ribbon.

He served as Eastern Air Line's Chief Pilot of Atlanta. Prior to his retirement in 1973, he flew the Lockheed L-1011, Eastern's largest equipment at that time. He was an admired and respected member of the management team during an impressive growth era of the company.

After retirement, Captain Bomar maintained a close association with the Retired Eastern Pilot's Association, serving as president in 1983. He worked on the REPA Convention Committee over a ten-year period and served as chairman several years; the last time was in 1990, not long before his final confinement. He died of cancer January 31, 1991, twelve days after Eastern landed for the last time. He never knew about the demise of the company, which meant so much to him. He served on the board of the Interfaith Chapel at Hartsfield International Airport and was made an honorary member of the Delta Pioneers, along with Birdie.

Birdie Bomar continues her association with Delta Air Lines through the retired stewardesses association, Clipped Wings. She is a former president of this organization and takes part in Delta's promotions, such as its fiftieth anniversary celebration. She is an active supporter of Delta's Retired Pilots Golden Wings Association.

She was made a member of the Eastern Air Lines Retirees Association, along with her late husband. She is a member of Eastern's Pilots' Wives Club, and continues her late husband's work for REPA, where she is known as its "Roving Ambassador." In recognition of her work in the early phases of the airline industry, she was awarded the Reader's Digest "Valiant Pioneers" award. Mrs. Bomar is also a member of the Retired Officers' Wives Club.

Birdie has now retired as a real estate agent with Northside Realty in Atlanta, where she worked for many years. She is now living in Marietta, Georgia in an assisted living facility.

Despite having a slight stroke, she continues to remain active and always captures the love and admiration of all who know her.

True to her unfailing devotion to the man she loved, when Dick entered Piedmont Hospital to spend the final months of his life, once again

Birdie, had a bed placed in his room (a real one this time) and maintained a constant vigil by his side until the end.

Following are excerpts from a eulogy written and read by a fellow pilot at the crowded funeral service for Captain Bomar, and one of his favorite poems.

IN MEMORIUM—DICK BOMAR
February 2, 1991

He lived by faith, and hope and love. He loved his God, his country, his company, his family and his friends.

He loved his God. Because of what he had seen, he had the faith to believe in those things he could not see. His strong faith carried him through a miserable war experience and later the loss of a leg. Many received inspiration from his courage and strength of character. Dick lived by the Golden Rule and went an extra mile if someone needed help. He used the talents God gave him to make life a little more comfortable for many.

He loved his country. Because of Dick's love for his country, he was not only patriotic, he wanted to serve his country. He became rated as a military pilot through his commercial flight experience and satisfied the academic requirements by correspondence courses. The U. S. Government did not spend a dime on his flight training.

Dick loved his company. Few pilots had reserved for them the opportunity of serving aviation in such a colorful and productive era.

Dick joined Eastern in 1940 and began flying the DC-2. He finished his career on the Lockheed 1011. His prior experience was in a true pioneer era where the pilot was the sole judge of the circumstances under which he discharged his duty, sustained the high honor of public service and brought reliability and dependability to advance aviation.

He had no equal with respect to achieving maximum co-operation and productivity from his flight crews and generated a spirit of great harmony and morale within the pilot ranks. To have completed a successful career encompassing an era from the fragile, fluttering fabric covered biplanes, exciting an adventurous public, to a highly developed transport technology system, which daily dispatches giant transports to foreign lands, places Dick alongside Eastern's giants.

Dick loved his family. Although he and Birdie had no children, they were especially close to their kinsmen and they provided guidance and aid to many young people in the family group. Birdie and Dick's marriage was a beautiful dove-tailing of mutual love, commitment and a merging of strength and understanding for almost 49 years.

Birdie was truly the wind beneath his wings and his reason for living.

He was her everything.

On any given day when the skies over Atlanta are blue, we can see the contrails of the great airliners of the world as they mark their path. These marks are soon swept away by the winds and time. Dick's flight through life leaves a mark that will never be swept away from our minds. His spirit will always remain with us and we will remember his last wish to his friends: "Love each other as I have loved you."

Captain Perry J. Hudson
Eastern Air Lines
Chief Pilot, Retired

Birdie
The True Story of Delta's First In-Air Stewardess

Birdie Bomar & Kathryn Bankston

High Flight
By
John Gillespie Magee, Jr.

Oh, I have slipped the surly bonds of earth
And danced the skies on laughter-silvered wings;
Sunward I've climbed, and joined the tumbling
mirth
Of sun-split clouds—and done a hundred things
You have not dreamed of—wheeled and soared
and swung
High in the sunlit silence. Hov'ring there,
I've chased the shouting wind along, and flung
My eager craft through footless halls of air.
Up, up the long, delirious, burning blue
Where never lark, or even eagle flew.
And, while with silent, lifting mind I've trod
The high untrespassed sanctity of space,
Put out my hand, and touched the face of God.

ABOUT THE AUTHOR

BIRDIE is Kathryn Dozier Bankston's first book. Her professional writing career began as a radio copywriter. She has done freelance writing for radio and print, including poems for special occasions. For ten years she had her own show on WGAU Radio, Athens, Georgia. While in Athens, she chaired the nationally recognized Radio-TV Institute sponsored by the Henry Grady School of Journalism and the Geargia Association of Broadcasters. She also hosted special TV programs on Channel 8. Kathryn came to Atlanta as one of the original staff members of WRNG Radio (now WCNN), where she hosted the "Call Kate Show", a two-hour daily talk program. She attended Agnes Scott College and received a Bachelor of Fine Arts degree from the University of Georgia. Upon graduation, she played the violin with the Atlanta Symphony Orchestra.

In 1986, she became a real estate agent with Northside Realty, where she met Birdie. Kathryn is currently with Jenny Pruitt & Associates Realtors. For thirty years, she has been a layreader at the episcopal Cathedral of St. Philip in Atlanta.

She recalls: "The inspiration for this book arose from sharing office duty with Birdie on a quiet Saturday afternoon when there were few telephone calls and Birdie started talking about her experiences as an airline stewardess. Before the afternoon was over, my sides ached from the exertion of continuous laughter."

I said, "Birdie, you ought to write a book." She responded, "That's what everybody says."

This book is the result of that delightful afternoon.

Printed in the United States
1771 6LVS00001B/43-207